BULGARIAN

Dictionary & Phrasebook

BULGARIAN
Dictionary & Phrasebook

Michaela Burilkovova

Hippocrene Books, Inc.
New York

For information, address:
HIPPOCRENE BOOKS, INC.
171 Madison Avenue
New York, NY 10016
www.hippocrenebooks.com

Library of Congress Cataloging-In-Publication Data

Burilkovova, Michaela.
Bulgarian dictionary & phrasebook : Bulgarian-English, English-Bulgarian /
Michaela Burilkovova.
p. cm.
Text in English and Bulgarian.
Includes bibliographical references.
ISBN 978-0-7818-1134-7 (pbk.)
ISBN 0-7818-1134-1 (pbk.)
1. Bulgarian language--Dictionaries--English. 2. English language--Dictionaries--Bulgarian. 3. Bulgarian language--Conversation and phrase books--English. 4. Bulgarian language--Spoken Bulgarian. I. Title. II. Title: Bulgarian dictionary and phrasebook. III. Title: English-Bulgarian dictionary and phrasebook.
PG979.B87 2012
491'.991321--dc23

2011046976

Many thanks to my husband Dimitri
and
to my two sons Alex and Denis

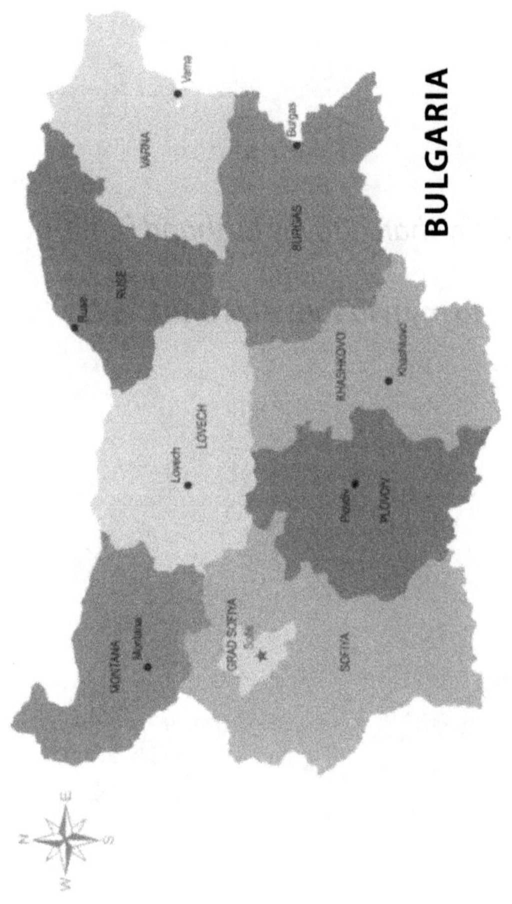
BULGARIA
VARNA
Varna
BURGAS
Burgas
RUSE
LOVECH
Lovech
KHASHKOVO
PLOVDIV
MONTANA
GRAD SOFIYA
SOFIYA
N
E
S
W

CONTENTS

Introduction 1
The Bulgarian Alphabet 9
Pronunciation Guide 11
A Basic Bulgarian Grammar 15
References 57
Abbreviations 58

BULGARIAN-ENGLISH DICTIONARY 59
ENGLISH-BULGARIAN DICTIONARY 117

PHRASEBOOK 179
- Etiquette & Basics 181
- Language 188
- Introductions 191
- Travel and Transportation 197
- Money 213
- Communications 215
- Accommodations 220
- Food & Drink 225

Shopping	233
Services	241
Culture & Entertainment	244
Sports	250
Health	253
Parts of the Body	261
Weather	263
Time	265
Colors	270
Numbers	271
Measurement & Conversion	273

INTRODUCTION

The Republic of Bulgaria is located in Southeast Europe in the eastern part of the Balkan Peninsula. It shares borders with Romania, Serbia, Macedonia, Greece, and Turkey, and is delimited by the Black Sea in the east. Founded in 681, Bulgaria is one of the oldest states in Europe. With a territory of 111,000 square kilometers (43,000 square miles), it is the sixteenth largest European state. The population is approximately 7.3 million. The capital and largest city is Sofia, situated near the western border at the foot of Mount Vitosha.

Slightly larger than the state of Tennessee, Bulgaria offers a large variation of landscapes for a country of its size: from the mild and sunny Black Sea coast with its golden sand resorts in the east, to fertile plains in the north and southeast, to several rugged mountainous chains with rich wildlife, excellent hiking trails and ski slopes. The mountain chains are: the Balkan Mountains (Stara Planina), splitting the country in two from west to east; the Rodopi chain in the south; and the Rila and Pirin mountains in the southwest, famous for their Alpine character, with many lakes and breathtaking vistas. The highest peak in the Balkan Peninsula, Musala (2925 m), is in the Rila Mountains.

Located at the crossroads of important routes from the West to the Middle East, and from North to South, the Bulgarian lands have been inhabited since the sixth millennia BC. The oldest treasure of golden jewels and artifacts in the world, from the fifth millennium BC, was found in the Varna Necropolis. Thracian tribes occupied the lands in the next several millennia, uniting in the Odrysian kingdom around the fifth century BC. The most famous Thracian is undoubtably Spartacus, a slave and gladiator who fought against the Romans so that he and the other slaves would be freed. Many traces from this period remain, like the Thracian tombs in Kazanlak and Sveshtari, both UNESCO World Heritage sites, and the Thracian Panagyurishte treasure, with its incomparable 24-karat gold rhytons (ceremonial drinking horns). Later the Thracians were conquered by Philip II of Macedon and his son, Alexander the Great, and by the Roman Empire. Probably the most famous relic of this era is the Roman Amphitheater in Plovdiv, built in the second century AD under Emperor Trajan. The Thracians mingled with and were assimilated by the South Slavic tribes moving in beginning in the sixth century AD.

The First Bulgarian Empire was founded in 681 AD by Khan (King) Asparukh, leader of Bulgarian tribes who came in from the plains north of the Black Sea. He united with the Slavs to win a decisive battle against Byzantium, followed by a peace treaty establishing the Bulgarian state with Pliska as the capital in modern northeast Bulgaria. Several of his successors played important roles in the development and expansion of the Bulgarian Empire. Tervel defeated a 26,000 strong Arab army in 717, stopping it from invading Central Europe. Krum introduced the first codes of law, valid both for Bulgars and Slavs, and won a decisive win in the battle of Pliska in 811, completely destroying the Byzantine army and killing Emperor Nicephorus I Genik. Boris I (the Baptist) introduced Christianity in 864, going away from the old deity Tangra. This started a rich tradition of religious visual arts, such as the icons, frescoes, and murals which can be found today in many well-preserved monasteries and churches in all parts of the country. He also introduced the oldest known Slavic alphabet, Glagolitic, which was used by the brothers Saints Cyril and Methodius in their missions to bring Christianity to the Southern Slavs. Later it was superseded by the Cyrillic alphabet (*azbuka*) developed by the disciples of Cyril and Methodius in the tenth century at the Preslav and Ohrid Literary Schools (Preslav succeeded Pliska as the capital). The Cyrillic alphabet and the Old Bulgarian language formed the basis for Church Slavonic, the *lingua franca* for Eastern Europe. The state reached its zenith under Emperor Simeon I, when Bulgaria was firmly established as the hub of a rich and varied Slavic Christian culture with large influence over Eastern Europe. The First Bulgarian Empire ended in 1018, when it fell under Byzantine rule.

The Second Bulgarian Empire was established in 1185, after a successful rebellion lead by the brothers Asen and Petar from the Asen dynasty which ruled Bulgaria for the next 70 years. Veliko Tarnovo was established as the capital, and many monuments from the Tarnovo artistic school remain. King Kaloyan fought the Knights of the Fourth Crusade and the recently formed Latin Empire, defeating them decisively in the battles of Adrianople (1205), when Emperor Baldwin I was captured and sent to Tarnovo, and Rusion (1206). The empire reached its peak under Ivan Asen II with rich culture and art, building of many new monasteries, minting of coins, trade expanding to Venice and Genoa, restoration of the Bulgarian Patriarchate, and organization of a navy.

In the fourteenth century, important divisions between the Bolyars, the nobility, weakened the country. The Bogomil heresy, founded in the tenth century by the priest Bogomil, was spreading, further weakening the state authority. The Second Empire ended in 1396, when Bulgaria was conquered by the Ottoman Turks. Bulgarians suffered many injustices under Ottoman rule, which lasted for almost five centuries. They were relegated to second-class citizens, and Bulgarian culture was isolated from Europe. The Bulgarian National Revival started in the second half of the eighteenth century with the works of the priest Saint Paisius of Hilendar, who wrote a "History of the Slav-Bulgarians," and opposed the Hellenization of Bulgarian language and culture.

This enlightment movement expanded quickly in the nineteenth century with the building of schools and churches and the writing of textbooks. The struggle for religious revival culminated with the creation of the Bulgarian Exarchate in 1870 by a Sultan edict, making the Bulgarian Orthodox church independent. The Patriarch in Constantinople reacted by excommunicating the Bulgarian Exarchate. After several unsuccessful uprisings, a large revolt in 1876 called the April Uprising was bloodily crushed, shocking civilized Europe. This led to the Russo-Turkish War of 1877-78 in which volunteer Bulgarian forces and the Romanian army also took part.

The Third Bulgarian State was established in 1878 with the Treaty of San Stefano. At the Berlin Congress the same year the Great Powers divided Bulgaria, bringing the southeast part back under formal Turkish rule. This part (Eastern Rumelia) was joined to the mainland in the act of Unification in 1885. Bulgaria became a constitutional monarchy under the quite liberal Tarnovo constitution in 1879 and Knyaz (Prince) Alexander I became the first head of state. Formal independence was declared in 1908 under King Ferdinand.

This period is marked by fast-paced modernization and expansion of cultural and trade ties with Europe. The first half of the twentieth century brought several bloody wars in the Balkans, and Bulgaria fought on the wrong side of history in both World Wars. Under King Boris III it regained control of Southern Dobrudzha through a treaty with Romania. Despite being forced to align with the Axis powers in World War II, Bulgaria declined to send military forces to the Eastern front. The entire Bulgarian Jewish population was saved by a strong public campaign, support from the Bulgarian Orthodox Church and a group of representatives, dispersing some families out of the capital of Sofia, outmaneuvering German demands, and finally the refusal of Boris III to extradite his citizens to concentration camps. In 1944 the Soviet Army entered Bulgaria, and Bulgarian forces joined the Allies for the rest of the war. Bulgaria came under the Soviet sphere of influence until 1989, when the communist regime lost its monopoly on power after the fall of the Berlin Wall.

The transition to a democratic state began with the first free elections in June of 1990, followed by the adoption of a new constitution the following year. Bulgaria is now a parliamentary democracy. The president is elected for five years and serves as head of state and commander in chief, with somewhat limited powers otherwise. The National Assembly, a single chamber parliament, consists of 240 deputies elected to four-year terms. Usually the leader of the majority party emerges as a prime minister, who heads the Council of Ministers which is charged with implementing the government's policies and laws. Bulgaria became a member of NATO in 2004 and joined the European Union in 2007.

Today the Republic of Bulgaria is completing its transition to a free market economy. After an economic crisis in the 1990s, Bulgaria is growing again. Sustained financial efforts and the introduction of a currency board restored fiscal discipline and the stability of the Bulgarian Lev. Now Bulgaria has one of the lowest levels of debt compared to GDP among European Union countries.

The Bulgarian language is a member of the South Slavic group from the Slavic family of languages that are part of the immense Indo-European language family. Indo-European languages are spoken by almost three billion native speakers. Bulgarian is also a member of the Balkan linguistic union and shares some characteristics with that group of languages. Noun inflections are strongly reduced in Bulgarian—while there are inflections for gender and number, there are no noun cases. Bulgarian has a suffixed definite article, setting it apart from most Slavic languages. It has lost the verb infinitive, while at the same time refining the verb system. The Cyrillic alphabet, also used in Russian and Ukrainian, was created in Bulgaria in the tenth century.

THE BULGARIAN ALPHABET

Bulgarian Letter	Romanization (English equivalent sounds)
А	[a]
Б	[b]
В	[v]
Г	[g]
Д	[d]
Е	[e]
Ж	[zh]
З	[z]
И	[i]
Й	[y]
К	[k]
Л	[l]
М	[m]
Н	[n]
О	[o]
П	[p]
Р	[r]
С	[s]
Т	[t]
У	[ou]
Ф	[f]
Х	[h]

Ц	[ts]
Ч	[ch]
Ш	[sh]
Щ	[sht]
Ъ	[u]
Ь	*special letter, used only in combination inside words*: ьо [yo]
Ю	[yu]
Я	[ya]

PRONUNCIATION GUIDE

а	**a** as in *arm*
б	**b** as in *bus*
в	**v** as in *via*
г	**g** as in *guy*
д	**d** as in *dish*
е	**e** as in *step*
ж	**s** as in *usual*
з	**z** as in *zebra*
и	**i** as in *sit*
й	**y** as in *youth*
к	**k** as in *king*
л	**l** as in *lion*
м	**m** as in *man*
н	**n** as in *no*
о	**o** as in *not*
п	**p** as in *pilot*
р	**r** as in *ring*
с	**s** as in *star*
т	**t** as in *tiger*
у	**ou** as in *tour*
ф	**f** as in *frog*
х	**h** as in *hair*
ц	**tz** as in *tzar*
ч	**ch** as in *chair*

ш	**sh** as in *ship*
щ	**sht** as in *shtick*
ъ	**u** as in *cut*
ьо	**yo** as in *canyon*
ю	**you** as in *you*
я	**ya** as in *yard*
дж	**j** as in *jazz*

The word accent in Bulgarian is varied. The stress is usually on the first or second syllable of a word. For example: *teacher* учител [ou'chitel]. There are some exceptions. The stress can be on the third syllable. For example: *continuation* продължение [produl'zhenie].

There are six vowels in Bulgarian. Depending on the position of the tongue they are divided into two groups:

low: **а, е, о**
high: **и, у, ъ**

Two diphthongs are typical for the Bulgarian language: **ю** and **я**. The former is a combination of **й** [y] and **у** [ou], the latter a combination of **й** [y] and **а** [a].

Bulgarian consonants have different phonetic pronunciation:

voiced: **б, в, г, д, ж, з, дж, дз**
voiceless: **п, ф, к, т, ш, с, х, ц, у, ч, щ**
sonor: **л, м, р, н, й, ь**

palatal: **р’, л’, м’, н’, б’, в’, о’, з’, дз’, г’, п’, ф’, т’, с’, ц’, к’, х’**

Voiced-voiceless consonant pairs: voiced consonants are pronounced as their voiceless counterparts at the end of words (the spelling remains the same).

б > [п]	зъ**б** [zup] *tooth*
в > [ф]	любо**в** [lyubof] *love*
г > [к]	дру**г** [drouk] *other*
д > [т]	гра**д** [grat] *town*
ж > [ш]	мъ**ж** [mush] *man*
з > [с]	мра**з** [mras] *freeze*

A BASIC BULGARIAN GRAMMAR

NOUNS & ARTICLES

The nouns in the Bulgarian language have the grammatical categories gender, number (singular and plural), definiteness, and case (only the vocative case). There are three genders of the nouns: masculine, feminine, and neuter (abbreviations: M., F., and N.). Bulgarian nouns can have suffixed articles after them. These are definite articles, pretty close to the use of ***the*** in English.

Examples for the singular:

masculine:
човек – човека – човекът
[chovek – choveka – chovekut]
man – the man

feminine:
жена – жената
[zhena – zhenata]
woman – the woman

neuter:
дете – детето
[dete – deteto]
child – the child

Example of plural:

студенти – студентите
[studenti – studentite]
students – the students

The Definite Article

The definite article depends on the gender and on the singular or plural form of the nouns. The masculine definite article has a full form and a shorter form. The full form is used for subjects and the short form for objects in the sentence. There is no such distinction for feminine and neuter, or in the plural, where there is just one form. This is a difficult area for non-native speakers and for the freshman student. The rules are followed more strictly in the written language; when spoken, the full form of the definite article is often replaced by the short form.

For masculine nouns that are in the singular and end in a hard consonant, the definite short article will be **-а** [a] and the full article will be **-ът** [ut]. For example:

двор – двора – дворът
[dvor – dvora – dvorut]
yard – the yard

човек – човека – човекът
[chovek – choveka – chovekut]
man – the man

If they end in a soft consonant (historically, in old Bulgarian), this softness is reflected in the article: short article is **-я** [ya] and full article is **-ят** [yat]. For example:

ден – деня – денят
[den – denya – denyat]
day – the day

This applies also to 'native' nouns ending in **-ар** and **-тел**. For example:

вестникар – вестникаря – вестникарят
[vestnikar – vestnikarya – vestnikayat]
newspaperman – the newspaperman

възпитател – възпитателя – възпитателят
[vuzpitatel – vuzpitatelya – vuzpitatelyat]
educator – the educator

For the plural in the masculine nouns the form is **-те** [te]:

мъж – мъже – мъжете
[muzh – muzhe – muzhete]
man – men – the men

The definite article comes after the changes required to form the plural. For the feminine nouns the definite article is **-та** [ta]:

жена – жената
[zhena – zhenata]
woman – the woman

For the neuter nouns it is **-то** [to]:

дете – детето
[dete – deteto]
child – the child

And for the plural feminine nouns it is **-те** [te]:

жени – жените
[zheni – zhenite]
women – the women

For the neuter plural nouns it is **-та** [ta]:
деца – децата
[detsa – detsata]
children – the children

The Indefinite Article

masculine: **един мъж** *a man*
feminine: **една жена** *a woman*
neuter: **едно дете** *a child*

The indefinite article specifies one from a group of many. The form changes depending on the noun's gender. The helping word in the singular has the form: for masculine gender **един** [edin] *a*, for feminine gender **една** [edna], and for the neuter gender **едно** [edno]. For example: **един мъж** [edin muzh], **една жена** [edna zhena], **едно дете**[edno dete]. For the plural: **едни мъже** [edni muzhe], **едни жени** [edni zheni], **едни деца** [edni detsa].

Formation of Nouns

Masculine

The masculine nouns generally end with a consonant in the singular. For example: **студент** [student] *student*, **чужденец** [chouzhdenets] *foreigner*. They are often formed by an adjective plus a suitable suffix at the end.

The first form of the suffix is **-ак, -як** [-ak, -yak]. For example:

дебел – дебелак [debel – debelak] *fat*

весел – веселяк [vesel – veselyak] *fun*

седем – седмак [sedem – sedmak] *seven*

Another suffix is **-ан,** for example:

голям – големан [golyam – goleman] *big*

A third group are the suffixes **-ар, -яр, -йар**, for example:

зидар [zidar] *bricklayer*
леяр [leyar] *steelworker*
ладийар [ladiyar] *boatman*

Widely used suffixes are **-тел**, for example:

учител [ouchitel] *teacher*

and **-ец**, for example

ловец [lovets] *hunter*

София – софиянец
[Sofia – sofiyanets]
Sofia – Sofian

The masculine nouns in plural have the ending **-и** [i]. For example:

приятел – приятели
[priyatel – priyateli]
friend – friends

театър – театри
[teatur – teatri]
theater – theaters.

Feminine

Feminine nouns are usually formed by the suffix **-ка** added to the masculine nouns. For these nouns the definite article is for example:

жена – жената
[zhena – zhenata]
woman – the woman

For the plural definite article form, for example:

жена – жени - жените
[zhena – zheni – zhenite]
woman – women – the women

For example:

masc.: **студент** [student] *student*
fem.: **студентка** [studentka]

masc.: **чужденец** [chouzhdenets] *foreigner*

fem.: **чужденка** [chouzhdenka]

There are also feminine nouns ending in **-я** [ya]. For example:

дьщеря [dushterya] *daughter*
леля [lelya] *aunt*

Nouns pertaining to plants and animals are also often feminine. For example:

котка [kotka] *cat*
риба [riba] *fish*
палма [palma] *palm*

Abstract nouns are also feminine. For example:

идея [ideya] *idea*
свобода [svoboda] *freedom*

The nouns ending in **-ост** [ost] and **-ест** [est] are also feminine. For example:

радост [radost] *joy*
свежест [svezhest] *freshness*

Neuter

Most neuter nouns end in **-е,** or **-о**:

ядене [yadene] *food*
колело [kolelo] *wheel, bicycle*

Neuter nouns also have definite articles. For example:

Singular:

дете – детето
[dete – deteto]
child – the child

Plural:

дете – деца – децата
[dete –detsa – detsata]
child – children – the children

Case of Nouns

In contrast to other Slavic languages, cases have almost disappeared in Bulgarian. Only the vocative case in nouns has remained. It means that you are calling somebody. For masculine nouns when they end in **-к** [k], **-х** [h], **- ж** [zh], **-ч** [ch], **-ш** [sh], **-ц** [ts], or when they take the suffix –**ин** [in] the vocative form ends in **-о** [o]. For example:

славянин [slavyanin] *Slav*
Славянино! [Slavyanino!]

мъж [muzh] *man*
Мъжо! [Muzho!]

американец [amerikanets] *American*
Американецо! [Amerikanetso!]

The nouns ending in **-й** [y], **-р** [r], **-л** [l] take the vocative form **-ю** [yu]. For example:

приятел [priyatel] *friend*
Приятелю! [Priyatelyu!]

The other nouns including personal nouns take the vocative form **-е** [e]. For example:

господин [gospodin] *sir*
Господине! [Gospodine!]

Тодор [Todor]
Тодоре! [Todore!]

When feminine nouns end in **-а** [a] and **-я** [ya] they take the vocative ending **-о** [o]. For example:

майка [mayka] *mother*
Майко! [Mayko!]

леля [lelya] *aunt*
Лельо! [Lelyo!]

сестра [sestra] *sister*
Сестро! [Sestro!]

жена [zhena] *woman*
Жено! [Zheno!]

Names ending in **-а** [a] and **-я** [ya] also form the vocative form with **-о** [o]. For example:

Мария [Mariya]
Марийо! [Mariyo!]

Елена [Elena]
Елено! [Eleno!]

Some feminine personal nouns ending in **-ка** [ka] or **-ица** [itsa] take the vocative form ending in **-е** [e]. For example:

Росица [Rositsa]
Росице! [Rositse!]

Diminutive Nouns

Diminutive nouns are formed by the suffixes **-че, -це, -ка** added to the nouns.

masc.: **брат – братче**
[brat – bratche]
brother

fem.: **жена – женичка**
[zhena – zhenichka]
woman

neut.: **коте – котенце**
[kote – kotentse]
cat – kitty

PERSONAL PRONOUNS

We will introduce the personal pronouns now because they are used in the conjugation of the verbs. As in English, they change depending on their role in the sentence (subject or object). In contrast to nouns, the nominative, accusative (direct complement), and dative (indirect complement) cases are used for personal pronouns.

Nom.	Acc.		Dat.	
	full form	*short form*	*full form*	*short form*
аз *I* [az]	**мене** [mene]	**ме** [me]	**на мене** [na mene]	**ми** *me* [mi]
ти *you* [ti]	**тебе** [tebe]	**те** [te]	**на тебе** [na tebe]	**ти** *you* [ti]
той *he* [toy]	**него** [nego]	**го** [go]	**на него** [na nego]	**му** *him* [mou]
тя *she* [tya]	**нея** [neya]	**я** [ya]	**на нея** [na neya]	**й** *her* [y]
то *it* [to]	**него** [nego]	**го** [go]	**на него** [na nego]	**му** *it* [mou]
ние *we* [nie]	**нас** [nas]	**ни** [ni]	**на нас** [na nas]	**ни** *us* [ni]
вие *you* [vie]	**вас** [vas]	**ви** [vi]	**на вас** [na vas]	**ви** *you* [vi]
те *they* [te]	**тях** [tyah]	**ги** [gi]	**на тях** [na tyah]	**им** *them* [im]

Reflexive:
себе (си) [sebe (si)] *myself, etc.*

VERBS

The loss of cases in Bulgarian has contributed to the development of a rich verb system, not very different from the English or French counterparts. Bulgarian verbs are inflected for person, number, and sometimes gender. There are nine tenses and the verbs have perfect and imperfect forms. The Bulgarian verb has lost its infinitive form — it is represented by the 1st person in the singular (sg.). In the Bulgarian language the subject personal pronouns are not obligatory and are often omitted when spoken. For the negative form, we add/put the particle **-не** [ne].

Present Tense

Auxiliary verb in infinitive form:
to be **съм** (irregular verb)

1st pers. sg. *I am* **аз съм** [az sum]
2nd pers. sg. *you are* **ти си**
3rd pers. sg. *he is* **той е**
she is **тя е**
it is **то е**

1st pers. pl. *we are* **ние сме**
2nd pers. pl. *you are* **вие сте**
3rd pers. pl. *they are* **те са**

Аз съм американец.
or
Американец съм.
I am American.

Ние сме тука.
or
Тука сме.
We are here.

Negative form for the verb *to be*: **аз съм**

1st pers. sg.	*I am not* **аз не съм** [az ne sum]
2nd pers. sg.	*you are not* **ти не си**
3rd pers. sg.	*he is not* **той не е**
	she is not **тя не е**
	it is not **то не е**
1st pers. pl.	*we are not* **ние не сме**
2nd pers. pl.	*you are not* **вие не сте**
3rd pers. pl.	*they are not* **те не са**

Иван не е в къщи.
[Ivan ne e v kushti.]
Ivan is not at home.

Ева не е ли тука?
[Eva na e li touka?]
Isn't Eva here?

Да, аз съм.
[Da, az sum.]
Yes, I am.

Не, (аз) не съм.
[Ne, (az) ne sum.]
No, I am not.

The regular form in present tense of auxiliary verb infinitive form:
to have **имам** [imam]

1st pers. sg.	*I have* **(аз) имам**
2nd pers. sg.	*you have* **(ти) имаш**
3rd pers. sg.	*he has* **той има**
	she has **тя има**
	it has **то има**

1st pers. pl.	*we have*	**(ние) имаме**
2nd pers. pl.	*you have*	**(вие) имате**
3rd pers. pl.	*they have*	**(те) имат**

(Аз) Имам молив.
[(Az) Imam moliv.]
I have a pencil.

Имате ли учебници?
[Imate li ouchebnitsi?]
Do you have textbooks?

Имаш ли химикалка?
[Imash li himikalka?]
Do you have a pen?

Negative form for the verb *to have*:

1st pers. sg.	*I have not*	**(аз) нямам**
2nd pers. sg.	*you have not*	**(ти) нямаш**
3rd pers. sg.	*he has not*	**той няма**
	she has not	**тя няма**
	it has not	**то няма**
1st pers. pl.	*we have not*	**(ние) нямаме**
2nd pers. pl.	*you have not*	**(вие) нямате**
3rd pers. pl.	*they have not*	**(те) нямат**

(Аз) Нямам кърпа за нос.
[(Az) Nyamam kurpa za nos.]
I don't have a handkerchief.

Имаш ли сапун?
[Imash li sapoun?]
Do you have soap?

The basic endings for the verbs in the present tense are given below. There are three main conjugations for the verbs in the present tense:

The first **e- conjugation**:

пиша [pisha] *write*

1st pers. sg.	**(аз) пиша** *I write*
2nd pers. sg.	**(ти) пишеш** *you write*
3rd pers. sg.	**той пише** *he writes*
	тя пише *she writes*
	то пише *it writes*
1st pers. pl.	**(ние) пишем** *we write*
2nd pers. pl.	**(вие) пишете** *you write*
3rd pers. pl.	**(те) пишат** *they write*

negation 1st pers. sg.:
не пиша [ne pisha], etc.

The second **и- conjugation**:

ходя [hodya] *walk*

1st pers. sg.	**(аз) ходя** *I walk*
2nd pers. sg.	**(ти) ходиш** *you walk*
3rd pers. sg.	**той ходи** *he walks*
	тя ходи *she walks*
	то ходи *it walks*
1st pers. pl.	**(ние) ходим** *we walk*
2nd pers. pl.	**(вие) ходите** *you walk*
3rd pers. pl.	**(те) ходят** *they walk*

negation 1st pers. sg.:
не ходя [ne hodya], etc.

The third **a- conjugation**:

гледам [gledam] *look* (*at*), *watch*

1st pers. sg.	**(аз) гледам** *I look* (*at*)
2nd pers. sg.	**(ти) гледаш** *you look* (*at*)
3rd pers. sg.	**той гледа** *he looks* (*at*)
	тя гледа *she looks* (*at*)
	то гледа *it looks* (*at*)
1st pers. pl.	**(ние) гледаме** *we look* (*at*)
2nd pers. pl.	**(вие) гледате** *you look* (*at*)
3rd pers. pl.	**(те) гледат** *they look* (*at*)

negation 1st pers. sg.:
не гледам [ne gledam], etc.

Verb Tenses of
съм *to be* and **имам** *to have*

Present Tense:
1st pers. sg. *I am* **(аз) съм** [(az) sum]

Past Tense (Perf./Imperf.):
1st pers. sg. *I was* **(аз) бях** [(az) byah]

Future tense:
1st pers. sg. *I will be, I shall be*
(аз) ще съм, ще бъда
[shte sum, shte buda]

Present tense:
1st pers. sg. *I have* **(аз) имам** [(az) imam]

Past tense (Perf./Imperf.):
1st pers. sg. *I had* **(аз) имах** [(az) imah]

Future tense:
1st pers. sg. *I will have* **(аз) ще имам**
[(az) shte imam]

Past Tense

Forms of **съм** [sum] *to be* in Past Tense — both perfect and imperfect:

1st pers. sg. **(аз) бях** [(az) byah] *I was*
2nd pers. sg. **(ти) бе/беше** *you were*
3rd pers. sg. **(той, тя, то) бе/беше** *he, she, it was*

1st pers. pl. **(ние) бяхме** *we were*
2nd pers. pl. **(вие) бяхте** *you were*
3rd pers. pl. **(те) бяха** *they were*

negation 1st pers. sg.:
(аз) не бях [(az) ne byah], etc. *I was not*

Past imperfect tense of **имам** *to have*:

1st pers. sg. **(аз) имах** [(az) imah] *I had*
2nd pers. sg. **(ти) имаше** *you had*
3rd pers. sg. **(той, тя, то) имаше** *he, she, it had*

1st pers. pl. **(ние) имахме** *we had*
2nd pers. pl. **(вие) имахте** *you had*
3rd pers. pl. **(те) имаха** *they had*

negation 1st pers. sg.:
(аз) нямах [(az) nyamah], etc.
I did not have

Past perfect tense of **имам** *to have*:

1st pers. sg. **(аз) имах** *I have had* [(az) imah]
2nd pers. sg. **(ти) има** *you have had*

3rd pers. sg. **(той, тя, то) има**
he, she, it have had

1st pers. pl. **(ние) имахме** *we have had*
2nd pers. pl. **(вие) имахте** *you have had*
3rd pers. pl. **(те) имаха** *they have had*

negation 1st pers. sg.:
(аз) нямах [(az) nyamah] *I have not had*

Verbal aspect – imperfect and perfect

The imperfect form of the verbs (abbreviation *imperf.*) expresses that the action is, was, or will be existing, without limitation in time. The English equivalents are present and continuous tenses and future tense with "*will be.*" This aspect can indicate future, present, or past. Example: **(аз) купувам** [(az) koupouvam] *to buy.*

The perfect form of the verbs (abbreviation *perf.*) corresponds roughly to the English perfect tense. These verbs cannot express the present, their present form expresses the future, and they also have past forms. Example: **купя** [koupya] *to buy.*

Concerning the past, the situation is more subtle and difficult for non-native speakers. The perfect tense expresses an action completed before the moment of speaking, in a defined point in the past. This is the main past tense used to express any past action, taken on its own, without regard for other past moments. It is used also to tell stories. The past imperfect, on the contrary, expresses an action that is not finished, or continues, relative to an orientation point in time (the moment spoken about).

Perfect verbs are often formed by adding prefixes to imperfect verbs:

imperfect (imperf.)		perfect (perf.)
плащам *to pay*	>	**заплащам**
питам се *to ask*	>	**запитвам се**
правя *to make*	>	**направя**
пия *to drink*	>	**изпия**

Past Perfect Tense

The first **e- conjugation**:

чета [cheta] *to read*

1st pers. sg.	**(аз) четох** *I have read* [(az) chetoh]
2nd pers. sg.	**(ти) чете** *you have read*
3rd pers. sg.	**(той, тя, то) чете** *he, she, it has read*
1st pers. pl.	**(ние) четохме** *we have read*
2nd pers. pl.	**(вие) четохте** *you have read*
3rd pers. pl.	**(те) четоха** *they have read*

negation 1st pers. sg.:
(аз) не четох [(az) ne chetoh]
I have not read, etc.

The second **и- conjugation**:

нося [nosya] *to carry*

1st pers. sg.	**(аз) носих** *I have carried* [(az) nosih]
2nd pers. sg.	**(ти) носи** *you have carried*
3rd pers. sg.	**(той, тя, то) носи** *he, she, it has carried*
1st pers. pl.	**(ние) носихме** *we have carried*
2nd pers. pl.	**(вие) носихте** *you have carried*
3rd pers. pl.	**(те) носиха** *they have carried*

negation 1st pers. sg.:
(аз) не носих [(az) ne nosih]
I have not carried, etc.

The third **a- conjugation**:

гледам [gledam] *to look* (*at*), *to watch*

1st pers. sg.	**(аз) гледах** *I have looked* (*at*) [(az) gledah]
2nd pers. sg.	**(ти) гледа** *you have looked* (*at*)
3rd pers. sg.	**(той, тя, то) гледа** *he, she, it has looked* (*at*)
1st pers. pl.	**(ние) гледахме** *we have looked* (*at*)
2nd pers. pl.	**(вие) гледахте** *you have looked* (*at*)

3rd pers. pl. **(те) гледаха**
they have looked (*at*)

negation 1st pers. sg.:
(аз) не гледах [(az) ne gledah]
I have not looked (*at*), etc.

Past Imperfect Tense

The first **е – conjugation**:

чета [cheta] *to read*

1st pers. sg. **(аз) четях** *I read*
[(az) chetyah]
2nd pers. sg. **(ти) четеше** *you read*
3rd pers. sg. **(той, тя, то) четеше**
he, she, it read

1st pers. pl. **(ние) четяхме** *we read*
2nd pers. pl. **(вие) четяхте** *you read*
3rd pers. pl. **(те) четяха** *they read*

negation 1st pers. sg.:
(аз) не четях [(az) ne chetyah]
I did not read, etc.

The second **и- conjugation**:

ходя [hodya] *to walk*

1st pers. sg. **(аз) ходех** *I walked*
[(az) hodeh]
2nd pers. sg. **(ти) ходеше** *you walked*
3rd pers. sg. **(той, тя, то) ходеше**
he, she, it walked

1st pers. pl. **(ние) ходехме** *we walked*
2nd pers. pl. **(вие) ходехте** *you walked*
3rd pers. pl. **(те) ходеха** *they walked*

negation 1st pers. sg.:
(аз) не ходех [(az) ne hodeh]
I did not walk, etc.

The third **a- conjugation**:

гледам [gledam] *to look* (*at*), *to watch*

1st pers. sg. **(аз) гледах** *I looked* (*at*) [(az) gledah]
2nd pers. sg. **(ти) гледаше** *you looked* (*at*)
3rd pers. sg. **(той, тя, то) гледаше** *he, she, it looked* (*at*)

1st pers. pl. **(ние) гледахме** *we looked* (*at*)
2nd pers. pl. **(вие) гледахте** *you looked* (*at*)
3rd pers. pl. **(те) гледаха** *they looked* (*at*)

negation 1st pers. sg.:
(аз) не гледах [(az) ne gledah]
I did not look (*at*), etc.

Past Indeterminate Tense (Perfect)

The past indeterminate tense is used to express an action completed at an unspecified moment in the past, the result of which is available at the moment of speaking, for example: **Чел съм тази книга.** [Chel sum tazi kniga.] *I have read this book.*

ходя [hodya] *to walk*

1st pers. sg.	**аз съм ходил** [az sum hodil] *or* **ходил съм** [hodil sum] *I have walked*
2nd pers. sg.	**ти си ходил** *or* **ходил си** *you have walked*
3rd pers. sg.	**той е ходил** *or* **ходил е** *he has walked* **тя е ходила** *or* **ходила е** *she has walked* **то е ходило** *or* **ходило е** *it has walked*
1st pers. pl.	**ние сме ходили** *or* **ходили сме** *we have walked*
2nd pers. pl.	**вие сте ходили** *or* **ходили сте** *you have walked*
3rd pers. pl.	**те са ходили** *or* **ходили са** *they have walked*

negation 1st pers. sg.:
(аз) не съм ходил [(az) ne sum hodil], etc.

Past Perfect (plus Quam Perfectum)

ходя [hodya] *to walk*

1st pers. sg.	**(аз) бях ходил** [(az) byah hodil] *I had walked*
2nd pers. sg.	**(ти) беше / бе ходил** *you had walked*
3rd pers. sg.	**(той) беше / бе ходил** *he had walked* **(тя) беше / бе ходила** *she had walked* **(то) беше / бе ходило** *it had walked*
1st pers. pl.	**(ние) бяхме ходили** *we had walked*
2nd pers. pl.	**(вие) бяхте ходили** *you had walked*
3rd pers. pl.	**(те) бяха ходили** *they had walked*

negation 1st pers. sg.:
(аз) не бях ходил
[(az) ne byah hodil]
I had not walked, etc.

Future Tense

Future tense is a two-word form, formed by the immutable particle (deriving from a verb) **ще** [shte] *will* and the present tense of the verb.

Future tense of **съм** *to be*:

1st pers. sg.	**(аз) ще съм** [(az) shte sum] *or* **(аз) ще бъда** [(az) shte buda] *I shall/will be*
2nd pers. sg.	**(ти) ще си** *or* **(ти) ще бъдеш** *you will be*
3rd pers. sg.	**(той, тя, то) ще е** *or* **ще бъде** *he, she, it will be*
1st pers. pl.	**(ние) ще сме** *or* **(ние) ще бъдем** *we shall/will be*
2nd pers. pl.	**(вие) ще сте** *or* **(вие) ще бъдете** *you will be*
3rd pers. pl.	**(те) ще са** *or* **(те) ще бъдат** *they will be*

negation 1st pers. sg.:
(аз) няма да бъда [(az) nyama da buda], etc.

Future tense of **имам** *to have*:

1st pers. sg.	**(аз) ще имам** *I will have*
2nd pers. sg.	**(ти) ще имаш** *you will have*
3rd pers. sg.	**(той, тя, то) ще има** *he, she, it will have*

1st pers. pl.	**(ние) ще имаме** *we will have*
2nd pers. pl.	**(вие) ще имате** *you will have*
3rd pers. pl.	**(те) ще имат** *they will have*

negation 1st pers sg.:
(аз) няма да имам
[(az) nyama da imam]
I will not have, etc.

Future imperf. **ходя** [hodya] *to walk*

1st pers. sg.	**(аз) ще ходя** [(az) shte hodya] *I will walk*
2nd pers. sg.	**(ти) ще ходиш** *you will walk*
3rd pers. sg.	**(той, тя, то) ще ходи** *he, she, it will walk*
1st pers. pl.	**(ние) ще ходим** *we will walk*
2nd pers. pl.	**(вие) ще ходите** *you will walk*
3rd pers. pl.	**(те) ще ходят** *they will walk*

negation 1st pers. sg.:
(аз) няма да ходя
[(az) nyama da hodya]
(аз) не ще ходя
[(az) ne shte hodya], etc.

Verbs with reflexive pronouns

Many verbs in Bulgarian are accompanied by the reflexive pronouns **се** or **си**. Sometimes their use (see examples below) can convey no particular meaning and be merely traditional. Or these verbs can be truly reflexive to express actions performed by the subject upon himself/ herself. And sometimes they express reciprocity (like *each other* or *one another*).

to wash myself	**къпя се** [kupya se]
to think	**мисля си** [mislya si]

питам се [pitam se] *to ask* (*myself*)
(present tense)

1st pers. sg.	**аз се питам** *or* **питам се** *I am asking*
2nd pers. sg.	**ти се питаш** *or* **питаш се** *you are asking*
3rd pers. sg.	**той, тя, то се пита** *or* **пита се** *he, she, it is asking*
1st pers. pl.	**ние се питаме** *or* **питаме се** *we are asking*
2nd pers. pl.	**вие се питате** *or* **питате се** *you are asking*
3rd pers. pl.	**те се питат** *or* **питат се** *they are asking*

negation 1st pers sg.:
(аз) не се питам [(az) ne se pitam]
I am not asking, etc.

Present Tense
1st pers. sg. *I am asking*
Аз се питам *or* **Питам се** etc.

Simple Past Tense:
1st pers. sg. *I asked*
Аз се питах *or* **Питах се**

Future Tense:
1st pers. sg. *I will ask*
Аз ще се питам *or* **Ще се питам**

Imperative:
Ask! **Ти питай!** *or* **Питай!**

Voice (Залог [zalog])

The Bulgarian language has two voices. Unlike in English (*I have driven home – I was driven home*), the auxiliary verb is always **съм** *to be*, the distinction is made by the form of the main verb.

Active voice (when the subject is performing the action). For example:

Чета книга. [Cheta kniga.]
I am reading a book.

Пиша речник. [Pisha rechnik.]
I am writing a dictionary.

Мия си ръцете. [Miya si rutsete.]
I am washing my hands.

Passive voice (the verb is in the passive voice when the action is performed on the subject). For example:

Книгата е прочетена.
[Knigata e prochetena.]
The book has been read.

Речникът се пише.
[Rechnikut se pishe.]
The dictionary is being written.

Ръцете се мият.
[Rutsete se miyat.]
The hands are being washed.

Mood of the Verb (Наклонение [naklonenie])

There are four moods in the Bulgarian language: indicative, re-narrated, imperative, and conditional.

Indicative Mood
Indicative is the main mood in a language, showing real actions being performed. It uses the forms of the verbs discussed so far. In addition, in Bulgarian with this mood the speaking person tells about an action that she had herself performed or witnessed. For example:

Тя чете тази книга.
[Tya chete tazi kniga.]
She is reading this book.

Re-narrated Mood
With the re-narrated mood the speaking person tells about an action that he has not witnessed himself. For example:

Той е чел тази книга.
[Toy e chel tazi kniga.]
He has (reportedly) read this book.

Imperative Mood
For imperative mood, the speaking person is commanding another person or persons. The imperative uses its own conjugation, by adding **-и** or **-ай** to the root of the verb for the singular form and **-ете** or **-айте** for the plural. For example:

Singular	**Plural**
чети! [cheti] *read*!	четете! [chetete!]
ходи! [hodi!] *walk*!	ходете! [hodete!]
гледай! [gleday!] *look*!	гледайте! [gledayte!]

Conditional Mood
The verb in conditional mood refers to an action that could happen at some present or future point in time. It is formed by the active past participle plus a special past form of the verb **съм** [sum] *to be*. For example:

(Аз) бих чел/а.
[(Az) bih chel/a.]
I would read.

ADJECTIVES

Adjectives in the Bulgarian language change their gender, number, and definiteness with the noun they relate to. They have separate forms for masculine, feminine, neuter, and plural. Usually adjectives are situated before the nouns.

m. sg. **нов молив** [nov moliv]
new pencil
f. sg. **нова кухня** [nova kouhnya]
new kitchen
n. sg. **ново легло** [novo leglo]
new bed
pl. **нови хотели** [novi hoteli]
new hotels

m. sg. **модерен хотел** [moderen hotel]
modern hotel
f. sg. **модерна пола** [moderna pola]
modern skirt
n. sg. **модерно палто** [moderno palto]
modern coat
pl. **модерни обувки** [moderni obouvki]
modern shoes

m. sg. **млад мъж** [mlad muzh]
young man
f. sg. **хубава жена** [houbava zhena]
pretty woman
n. sg. **чаровно дете** [charovno dete]
charming child

m. pl. **млади мъже** [mladi muzhe]
young men

f. pl. **хубави жени** [houbavi zheni] *pretty women*

n. pl. **чаровни деца** [charovni detsa] *charming children*

Formation of adjectives with suffix **-ски**

m. sg. **английски чай** [angliyski chay] *English tea*

f. sg. **английска мода** [angliyska moda] *English fashion*

n. sg. **английско ядене** [angliysko yadene] *English meal*

pl. **английски чайове** [angliyski chayove] *English teas*

The comparative is formed with the particle **по-** [po-]. The superlative is formed with the particle **най-** [nay-].

better

m. sg. **по-добър** [po-dobur]
f. sg. **по-добра** [po–dobra]
n. sg. **по-добро** [po–dobro]
pl. **по-добри** [po–dobri]

best

m.sg. **най-добър** [nay–dobur]
f. sg. **най-добра** [nay–dobra]
n. sg. **най-добро** [nay–dobro]
pl. **най-добри** [nay–dobri]

To form the definite form suffixes are added after the adjective. For the masculine adjective the short form is **-я** and the full form is **-ят**. For example: **добър човек – добрия човек** [dobur chovek – dobriya chovek] *good man – a good man*; **добрият човек** [dobriyat chovek] *the good man* (when subject in the sentence). Note that when the definiteness is expressed through the adjective, the noun in its basic form is used (no double counting). For the feminine adjective the definite article is **-та**. For example: **добрата жена** [dobrata zhena] *the good woman*. For the neuter adjective the definite article is **-то**. For example: **доброто дете** [dobroto dete] *the good child.*

You can use two or more adjectives in a sentence. For example:

> **(Аз) имам нов и хубав пуловер.**
> [(Az) imam nov i houbav poulover.]
> *I have a new and nice sweater.*

PRONOUNS

The pronouns in Bulgarian vary with gender, number, definiteness, and case.

Possessive Pronouns

	Full Form				Short Form
	M.	F.	N.	Pl.	
my	**мой**	**моя**	**мое**	**мои**	**ми**
	[moy]	[moya]	[moe]	[moi]	[mi]
yours	**твой**	**твоя**	**твое**	**твои**	**ти**
	[tvoy]	[tvoya]	[tvoe]	[tvoi]	[ti]
his	**негов**	**негова**	**негово**	**негови**	**му**
	[negov]	[negova]	[negovo]	[negovi]	[mou]
her	**неин**	**нейна**	**нейно**	**нейни**	**й**
	[nein]	[neyna]	[neyno]	[neyni]	[y]
its	**негов**	**негова**	**негово**	**негови**	**му**
	[negov]	[negova]	[negovo]	[negovi]	[mou]
our	**наш**	**наша**	**наше**	**наши**	**ни**
	[nash]	[nasha]	[nashe]	[nashi]	[ni]
your	***ваш**	**ваша**	**ваше**	**ваши**	**ви**
	[vash]	[vasha]	[vashe]	[vashi]	[vi]
their	**техен**	**тяхна**	**тяхно**	**техни**	**им**
	[tehen]	[tyahna]	[tyahno]	[tehni]	[im]

Reflexive:

your own

	свой	**своя**	**свое**	**свои**	**си**
	[svoy]	[svoya]	[svoe]	[svoi]	[si]

---

*The possessive pronouns **Ваш** [Vash] *your* in the Bulgarian language is sometimes capitalized. The capitalized form is used when addressing someone politely.

These pronouns also have definite articles that are placed after them like a suffix. For example:

my – our:
m. **мой – моят**
f. **моя – моята**
n. **мое – моето**
pl. **мои – моите**

Interrogative Pronouns

	M.	F.	N.	Pl.
who	**кой**	**коя**	**кое**	**кои**
	[koy]	[koya]	[koe]	[koi]
what	**какъв**	**каква**	**какво**	**какви**
	[kakuv]	[kakva]	[kakvo]	[kakvi]
whose	**чий**	**чия**	**чие**	**чии**
	[chiy]	[chiya]	[chie]	[chii]

The definite article is placed after the interrogative pronouns like a suffix. For example:

m. **кой – който**
f. **коя – която**
n. **кое – което**
pl. **кои – които**

Relative Pronouns

	M.	F.	N.	Pl.
which	**който**	**която**	**което**	**които**
	[koyto]	[koyato]	[koeto]	[koito]
what /	**какъвто**	**каквато**	**каквото**	**каквито**
whatever	[kakuvto]	[kakvato]	[kakvoto]	[kakvito]
whose	**чийто**	**чиято**	**чието**	**чиито**
	[chiyto]	[chiyato]	[chieto]	[chiito]

Demonstrative Pronouns

	M.	F.	N.	Pl.
this	**този**	**тази**	**това**	**тези** (*these*)
	[tozi]	[tazi]	[tova]	[tezi]
that	**онзи**	**онази**	**онова**	**онези** (*those*)
	[onzi]	[onazi]	[onova]	[onezi]
such	**такъв**	**такава**	**такова**	**такива**
	[takuv]	[takava]	[takova]	[takiva]

Indefinite Pronouns

	M.	F.	N.	Pl.
somebody				
	някой	**някоя**	**някое**	**някои**
	[nyakoy]	[nyakoya]	[nyakoe]	[nyakoi]
someone				
	някакъв	**някаква**	**някакво**	**някакви**
	[nyakakuv]	[nyakakva]	[nyakakvo]	[nyakakvi]
someone's				
	нечий	**нечия**	**нечие**	**нечии**
	[nechiy]	[nechiya]	[nechie]	[nechii]
some, several				
	няколко			
	[nyakolko]			

Reflexive Pronouns

Personal reflexive pronouns have accusative and dative forms:

myself, to myself, etc.

	Accusative	Dative
Full form	**себе си**	**на себе си**
	[sebe si]	[na sebe si]
Short form	**се** [se]	**си** [si]

Possessive reflexive pronouns are used when the subject owns the object, for example, *I see my sister*.

	M	F	N	Pl.	Short
my, etc.	**свой**	**своя**	**свое**	**свои**	**си**
	[svoi]	[svoya]	[svoe]	[svoi]	[si]

Negative Pronouns

Negative pronouns are formed by the interrogative plus the prefix **ни-** [ni].

	M.	F.	N.	Pl.
no one, nobody				
	никой	**никоя**	**никое**	**никои**
	[nikoy]	[nikoya]	[nikoe]	[nikoi]
none				
	никакъв	**никаква**	**никакво**	**никакви**
	[nikakuv]	[nikakva]	[nikakvo]	[nikakvi]
nobody's				
	ничий	**ничия**	**ничие**	**ничии**
	[nichiy]	[nichiya]	[nichie]	[nichii]
none, not any				
	николко			
	[nikolko]			

ADVERBS

In the Bulgarian language most adverbs are formed from the singular neuter form of adjectives. For example:

бавно [bavno] *slowly*
ниско [nisko] *low*
внимателно [vnimatelno] *carefully*
обикновено [obiknoveno] *usually*

If the masculine form of the adjective ends in **-ски** or **-ки**, it is used instead, for example:

майсторски [maystorski] *skillfully*

A second group of adverbs are words specifying place, time, manner, quality, and degree. Some are original words; others were derived from case forms no longer in use.

Adverbs of place:
тук [touk] *here*
къде? [kude?] *where*?
долу [dolou] *down*

Temporal adverbs:
кога? [koga?] *when*?
утре [outre] *tomorrow*
сега [sega] *now*

Adverbs of manner:
как? [kak?] *how*?
добре [dobre] *well*
зле [zle] *bad*

Adverbs of degree:
много [mnogo] *much*
доста [dosta] *quite*
почти [pochti] *almost*
твърде [tvurde] *too*
толкова [tolkova] *so*

Спирката е тук.
[Spirkata e touk.]
The station is here.

Утре заминаваме.
[Outre zaminavame.]
We are departing tomorrow.

Как си?
[Kak si?]
How are you?

Много добре.
[Mnogo dobre.]
Very well.

Почти тук.
[Pochti touk.]
Almost here.

SYNTAX

The Bulgarian language has two basic sentence items—subject and predicate. This is the basic syntactical pair. For example:

Фермерите работят.
[Fermerite rabotyat.]
The farmers are working.

The masculine plural noun **фермерите** *farmers* is the subject and the 3rd person plural verb **работят** *are working* is the predicate.

Момичето спи.
[Momicheto spi.]
The girl is sleeping.

The feminine singular noun **момиче** *girl* is the subject and the 3rd person singular verb **спи** *is sleeping* is the predicate.

(Аз) Имам книга.
[(Az) Imam kniga.]
I have a book.

Here the 1st person singular verb **имам** *have* is the predicate and **книга** *book* is the object, but the subject is missing. This is a *subjectless* sentence, typical for the Bulgarian language. For example:

Топло е. *It is warm.*
Вали. *It is raining.*
Горещо е. *It is hot.*
Вали сняг. *It is snowing.*
Студено е. *It is cold.*
Замръзва. *It is freezing.*
Свободно ли е там? *Is it free there*?
Тука е свободно. *It is free here.*

SUBJECT AND OBJECT

In English the difference between subject and object is expressed by the word order (subject followed by the object). Interestingly, in the Bulgarian language the word order, while more often than not still the same, plays a much more limited role in expressing this difference. This is even more remarkable if one takes into account that there are almost no noun cases. The relationship is conveyed by the agreement between the subject and the verb in the sentence (which changes with the person). As a result the word order is rather free. The only ambiguity arises when both subject and object are in the third person. Then a construct called clitic doubling (full nouns and clitic pronouns for them appearing in the same verb phrase) sometimes comes to the rescue, especially in the spoken language. In Bulgarian, when the meaning is clear from the context, even this can be omitted. Some examples:

(*I*) *met Ivan.*

Срещнах Иван.
[Sreshtnah Ivan.]
(*usual form*)

Иван срещнах.
[Ivan sreshtnah.]
(*tends to put more emphasis on the subject*)

Иван (го) срещнах.
[Ivan (go) sreshtnah.]
(*same as above, makes it very clear by using the personal clitic [unstressed] pronouns:* **го, я, ги** *[go, ya, gi]* him, her, them)

Here the verb form (first person singular) makes it clear that "*I*" is the subject in all variations.

Below is an example where the doubling is needed to determine the subject. As discussed already, this is only necessary when both subject and object are in the third person. The main features of the doubled object are: 1) it comes first, taking the place normally occupied by the subject, 2) it usually is in the definite form, and 3) it does not get the logical stress.

Две овце ги изяли вълците.
[Dve ovtse gi izyali vultsite.]
The wolves ate two sheep.
(Literally: *Two sheep them ate the wolves.*)

The double subject is: **две овце** *two sheep* + **ги** *them*. If we omit the pronoun **ги** the sentence becomes:

Две овце изяли вълците.
Two sheep ate the wolves.

REFERENCES

Проф. Любомир Андрейчин, проф. Константин Попов, проф.Стоян Стоянов, „Граматика на българския език". Sofia, 1977, Изд. № 20548.

Снежана Бояджиева, Лена Илиева, „Англо – Български и Българско-Английски речник". ABAGAR, Veliko Turnavo, ISBN 954-9607-65-8.

The Merriam-Webster Dictionary. 2004, ISBN 978-0-87779-930-6.

The Merriam-Webster Thesaurus. 2005, ISBN-10: 0-87779-850-8.

Ivan Tchomakov, *Bulgarian-English/ English-Bulgarian Practical Dictionary*. New York, Hippocrene Books, fifth printing, 2004, ISBN 0-87052-145-4.

Michaela Burilkovova, *Czech-English/ English-Czech Dictionary and Phrasebook*. New York, Hippocrene Books, 2003, ISBN 0-7818-0942-8.

Bulgarian Phrasebook, Second edition, edited by Liudmil Tsvetkov, cover design by Kassimir Kotsev. ABAGAR, Veliko Turnovo, ISBN 954-8805-23-5.

Marc Lester, *McGraw-Hill's Essential ESL Grammar*. McGraw-Hill 2008, ISBN-10: 0-07-149642-4.

ABBREVIATIONS USED IN DICTIONARY

adj.	adjective
adv.	adverb
conj.	conjunction
F.	feminine
gram.	grammatical
imperf.	imperfect (for verbs)
interj.	interjection
M.	masculine
N.	neuter
n.	noun
num.	number
п.	case (in Bulgarian, падеж [padezh])
part.	particle
perf.	perfect (for verbs)
pers.	person
pl.	plural
prep.	preposition
pron.	pronoun
sg.	singular
v.	verb

BULGARIAN–ENGLISH DICTIONARY

A

а [a] *conj.* and
абсолютно [absolyutno] *adv.* absolutely
август [avgust] *n.* August
автобус [avtobus] *n.* bus
автомобил [avtomobil] *n.* automobile, car
автор [avtor] *n.* author
агенция [agentsiya] *n.* agency
агне [agne] *n.* lamb
адвокат [advokat] *n.* lawyer
администрация [administratsiya] *n.* administration
адрес [adres] *n.* address
аз [az] *pron.* I
азбука [azbouka] *n.* alphabet
академически [akademicheski] *adj.* academic
ако [ako] *conj.* if
акт [akt] *n.* act
актив [aktiv] *n.* asset
активен [aktiven] *adj.* active
активност [aktivnost] *n.* activity
акция [aktsiya] *n.* action
акция (борсова) [aktsiya (borsova)] *n.* share (stock exchange)
алтернативен [alternativen] *adj.* alternative
амбиция [ambitsiya] *n.* aspiration
американец [amerikanets] *n.* American
американски [amerikanski] *adj.* American
анализ [analiz] *n.* analysis
анализирам [analiziram] *v.* analyze
ананас [ananas] *n.* pineapple
английски [angliyski] *adj.* English

анонсирам [anonsiram] *v.* announce
апартамент [apartament] *n.* apartment
апел [apel] *n.* appeal
апелирам [apeliram] *v.* appeal
април [april] *n.* April
аптека [apteka] *n.* drugstore, pharmacy
аранжирам [aranzhiram] *v.* arrange
армия [armiya] *n.* army
асансьор [asansyor] *n.* lift, elevator
асоциация [asotsiatsiya] *n.* association
аспект [aspekt] *n.* aspect
атака [ataka] *n.* attack
атмосфера [atmosfera] *n.* atmosphere
атрактивен [atraktiven] *adj.* attractive

Б

бавен [baven] *adj.* slow
бакалница [bakalnitsa] *n.* grocery
бактерия [bakteriya] *n.* bacteria
бакшиш [bakshish] *n.* tip
балкон [balkon] *n.* balcony
банален [banalen] *adj.* banal
банан [banan] *n.* banana
банка [banka] *n.* bank
банкет [banket] *n.* banquet
банкнота [banknota] *n.* banknote, bill
баня [banya] *n.* bathroom, bath
бароков [barokov] *adj.* baroque
басейн [baseyn] *n.* swimming pool
баскетбол [basketbol] *n.* basketball
басня [basnya] *n.* fable
баща [bashta] *n.* father
бебе [bebe] *n.* baby
беда [beda] *n.* trouble
без [bez] *prep.* without

безопастност [bezopasnost] *n.* security
безпокоя [bezpokoya] *v.* disturb
безработица [bezrabotitsa] *n.* unemployment
бележка [belezhka] *n.* note
бензин [benzin] *n.* gasoline
библиотека [biblioteka] *n.* library
бивш [bivsh] *adj.* former
бизнес [biznes] *n.* business
билет [bilet] *n.* ticket
билярд [bilyard] *n.* billiards
бинокъл [binokul] *n.* binocular
биография [biografiya] *n.* biography
бира [bira] *n.* beer
бисквита [biskvita] *n.* cookie
бистър [bistur] *adj.* clear
бих могъл [bih mogul] *v.* might
благодарен [blagodaren] *adj.* grateful
благодарност [blagodarnost] *n.* thanks
благодаря [blagodarya] *v.* thank
блестя [blestya] *v.* glance, shine, sparkle
блуза [blouza] *n.* blouse
боб [bob] *n.* bean
боклук [boklouk] *n.* garbage
болен [bolen] *n.* sick
болен [bolen] *adj.* ill
болка [bolka] *n.* pain
болница [bolnitsa] *n.* hospital
бонбон [bonbon] *n.* candy
борба [borba] *n.* fight
боря се [borya se] *v.* fight
боя [boya] *n.* paint
боядисвам [boyadisvam] *v.* paint
брада [brada] *n.* chin; beard
браня [branya] *v.* defend
брат [brat] *n.* brother
брашно [brashno] *n.* flour

бръснар [brusnar] *n.* barber
буза [bouza] *n.* cheek
букет [bouket] *n.* bouquet
бутам [boutam] *v.* push
бутилка [boutilka] *n.* bottle
бъбрек [bubrek] *n.* kidney
бъдещ [budesht] *adj.* future
бъдеще [budeshte] *n.* future
България [Bulgariya] *n.* Bulgaria
български [bulgarski] *adj.* Bulgarian
бърз [burz] *adj.* fast, quick
бърза помощ [burza pomosht] *n.* ambulance; first aid
бързам [burzam] *v.* hurry
бързане [burzane] *n.* hurry
бързо [burzo] adv. quickly, rapidly
бюро [byuro] *n.* bureau, agency
бюст [byust] *n.* breast
бягане [byagane] *n.* run
бягство [byagstvo] *n.* escape
бял [byal] *adj.* white
бял дроб [byal drob] *n.* lung

В

в [v] *prep.* in, into, at
в основата си [v osnovata si] *adv.* basically
важен [vazhen] *adj.* important
важност [vazhnost] *n.* importance
ваза [vaza] *n.* vase
ваканция [vakantsiya] *n.* vacation
ваксинация [vaksinatsiya] *n.* vaccination
вана [vana] *n.* bathtub
вариация [variatsiya] *n.* variation
вариете [variete] *n.* variety
варя [varya] *v.* boil

ваш [vash] *adj.* your
ваш [vash] *pron.* yours
вдигам [vdigam] *v.* raise
веднага [vednaga] *adv.* immediately
Великден [Velikden] *n.* Easter
вена [vena] *n.* vein
вентилатор [ventilator] *n.* fan
верижка [verizhka] *n.* chain
вестник [vestnik] *n.* newspaper
ветрило [vetrilo] *n.* fan
вече [veche] *adv.* already, yet
вечер [vecher] *n.* evening
вечеря [vecherya] *n.* dinner, supper
вечерям [vecheryam] *v.* dine
вземам [vzemam] *v.* take
вид [vid] *n.* sort, kind; article
вие [vie] *pron.* you
виждам [vizhdam] *v.* see
вик [vik] *n.* cry
викам [vikam] *v.* call, shout
вина [vina] *n.* blame
винаги [vinagi] *adv.* always
вино [vino] *n.* wine
висок [visok] *adj.* tall, high
високо [visoko] *adv.* high, highly
височина [visochina] *n.* height
включвам [vklyuchvam] *v.* include, involve, incorporate
включително [vklyuchitelno] *prep.* including
вкус [vkous] *n.* taste
вкусвам [vkousvam] *v.* taste
влак [vlak] *n.* train
власт [vlast] *n.* authority, power
влизам [vlizam] *v.* come in
влизане [vlizane] *n.* entry
влияние [vliyanie] *n.* influence

влияя [vliyaya] *v.* influence
вместо [vmesto] *adv.* instead
внимание [vnimanie] *n.* attention
внимателен [vnimatelen] *adj.* cautious
вода [voda] *n.* water
водя [vodya] *v.* guide, lead, head
война [voyna] *n.* war
войник [voynik] *n.* soldier
войска [voyska] *n.* army
впечатление [vpechatlenie] *n.* impression
вписвам [vpisvam] *v.* list
врат [vrat] *n.* neck
врата [vrata] *n.* gate, door
време [vreme] *n.* weather; time
връзвам [vruzvam] *v.* bind, tie
връзка [vruzka] *n.* relationship
връщане [vrushtane] *n.* return
врял [vryal] *adj.* boiling
все още [vse oshte] *adv.* still
всеки ден [vseki den] *adj.* everyday
всеки [vseki] *adj.* each, every
всичко [vsichko] *adj.* all
всъщност [vsushnost] *adv.* actually
всякакъв [vsyakakuv] *adj.* any
втори [vtori] *adj.* second
вторник [vtornik] *n.* Tuesday
вход [vhod] *n.* entrance, gate
вчера [vchera] *adv.* yesterday
въвеждам [vuvezhdam] *v.* introduce
въглища [vuglishta] *n. pl.* coal
възхищавам се [vuzhishtavam se] *v.* admire
възглавница [vuzglavnitsa] *n.* pillow
възглавявам [vuzglavyavam] *v.* head
въздействам [vuzdeystvam] *v.* influence, affect
въздух [vuzdouh] *n.* air

възможен [vuzmozhen] *adj*. possible, potential
възможност [vuzmozhnost] *n*. chance, opportunity, possibility
възнамерявам [vuznamerjavam] *v*. intend, mean
възраст [vuzrast] *n*. age
възрастен [vuzrasten] *adj*. adult
възстановявам [vuzstanovyavam] *v*. recover
вълна [vulna] *n*. wool
вълна (във водата) [vulna (vuv vodata)] *n*. wave (on the water)
вън [vun] *adv.* out
въобще [vuobshte] *adv*. at all
въпреки това [vupreki tova] *adv*. nevertheless
въпреки че [vupreki che] *conj*. although
въпрос [vupros] *n*. question; affair
въртя (се) [vurtya (se)] *v*. turn (around), rotate
вътре [vutre] *adv., prep.* in, inside
вътрешен [vutreshen] *adj*. internal, inner
вътрешно [vutreshno] *adv*. inside
вяра [vyara] *n*. faith
вятър [vyatur] *n*. wind

Г

газ [gaz] *n*. gas
гараж [garazh] *n*. garage
генерал [general] *n*. general
генерален [generalen] *adj*. general
генерация [generatsiya] *n*. generation
генерирам [generiram] *v*. generate
ги [gi] *pron*. them
гид [gid] *n*. guide, tour guide

глава [glava] *n.* head; chapter
главен [glaven] *adj.* main, prime
глагол [glagol] *n. gram.* verb
глад [glad] *n.* famine, hunger
гладя [gladya] *v.* iron
глас [glas] *n.* voice
гласувам [glasouvam] *v.* vote
гласуване [glasouvane] *n.* vote
гледам [gledam] *v.* look, view
гледка [gledka] *n.* view
говеждо месо [govezhdo meso] *n.* beef
говоря [govorya] *v.* talk, converse, speak
година [godina] *n.* year
годишен [godishen] *adj.* annual
годишно време [godishno vreme] *n.* season
гол [gol] *n.* goal (sports)
голям [golyam] *adj.* big, large, great
гора [gora] *n.* woods, forest
горд [gord] *adj.* proud
горен [goren] *adj.* upper
горчив [gorchiv] *adj.* bitter
господар [gospodar] *n.* lord
господин [gospodin] *n.* sir
господин (г-н) [gospodin (g-n)] *n.* Mister (Mr.)
госпожа [gospozha] *n.* madam, lady
госпожа (г-жа) [gospozha (g-zha)] *n.* Missus (Mrs.)
госпожица (г-ца) [gospozhitsa (g-tsa)] *n.* Miss
гост [gost] *n.* guest
готвя [gotvya] *v.* cook
готин [gotin] *adj. slang* cute, cool
готически [goticheski] *adj.* Gothic
готов [gotov] *adj.* ready

град [grad] *n.* town, city
градина [gradina] *n.* garden
градски [gradski] *adj.* urban
градски център [gradski tsentur] *n.* downtown
гражданин [grazhdanin] *n.* citizen
граматически [gramaticheski] *adj.* grammatical
граница [granitsa] *n.* limit, border
гребен [greben] *n.* comb
грешен [greshen] *adj.* wrong; sinful
грешка [greshka] *n.* mistake
гривна [grivna] *n.* bracelet, bangle
грижа [grizha] *n.* concern, care
грижа се [grizha se] *v.* care, provide
грозде [grozde] *n.* grape
грозен [grozen] *adj.* ugly
група [groupa] *n.* group
гръб [grub] *n.* back
гръбначен стълб [grubnachen stulb] *n.* backbone
губя [goubya] *v.* lose
гулаш [goulash] *n.* goulash
гума [gouma] *n.* tire
гъба [guba] *n.* mushroom
гънка [gunka] *n.* fold
гърло [gurlo] *n.* throat

Д

да [da] *adv.* yes
давам [davam] *v.* grant, give
далеко [daleko] *adv.* far, away
далеч [dalech] *adv.* far, away
далечен [dalechen] *adj.* faraway
данък [danuk] *n.* tax
дарявам [daryavam] *v.* donate

дата [data] *n.* date
два пъти [dva puti] *adv.* twice
две [dve] *num.* two
движа се [dvizha se] *v.* move
движение [dvizhenie] *n.* movement
двоен [dvoen] *adj.* double
двор [dvor] *n.* yard
дебел [debel] *adj.* fat, thick
девет [devet] *num.* nine
действам [deystvam] *v.* act
действие [deystvie] *n.* act
действителен [deystvitelen] *adj.* actual
декември [dekemvri] *n.* December
деля [delya] *v.* divide
ден [den] *n.* day
депозит [deposit] *n.* deposit
десерт [desert] *n.* dessert
десет [deset] *num.* ten
детайл [detail] *n.* detail
дете [dete] *n.* kid, child
деятел [deyatel] *n.* agent, functionary
джентълмен [dzhentulmen] *n.* gentleman
джоб [dzhob] *n.* pocket
диария [diariya] *n.* diarrhea
диета [dieta] *n.* diet
дизайн [dizayn] *n.* design
директор [direktor] *n.* principle, director
дискета [disketa] *n.* diskette
дискусия [diskousiya] *n.* debate, dispute
дишане [dishane] *n.* breath
дневен ред [dneven red] *n.* agenda
дневник [dnevnik] *n.* diary
днес [dnes] *adv.* today
добавка [dobavka] *n.* addition
добре [dobre] *interj.* okay
добре [dobre] *adv.* well

добро [dobro] *n.* good
добър [dobur] *adj.* good
доверие [doverie] *n.* trust, faith
доверявам се [doveryavam se] *v.* trust
довиждане [dovizhdane] *interj.* good-bye
довод [dovod] *n.* argument, reason
доволен [dovolen] *adj.* glad, pleased
договор [dogovor] *n.* contract
доказателство [dokazatelstvo] *n.* evidence
доказвам [dokazvam] *v.* prove
докато [dokato] *prep.* until
доклад [doklad] *n.* report
докосвам [dokosvam] *v.* touch
долу [dolou] *adv.* down
домакинство [domakinstvo] *n.* household
домат [domat] *n.* tomato
домашен [domashen] *adj.* domestic
домашни птици [domashni ptitsi] *n.* poultry
донасям [donasyam] *v.* bring, fetch
допир [dopir] *n.* touch
допълнение [dopulnenie] *n.* addition
допълнителен [dopulnitelen] *adj.* additional, complementary
достигам [dostigam] *v.* reach
достойнство [dostoynstvo] *n.* dignity
достъп [dostup] *n.* access
достъпен [dostupen] *adj.* available
доктор [doktor] *n.* doctor
доход [dohod] *n.* income
драг [drag] *adj.* dear
древен [dreven] *adj.* ancient
друг [droug] *pron.* other; *adj.* else, other

дупка [doupka] *n.* hole, gap
дъвча [duvcha] *v.* chew
дъжд [duzhd] *n.* rain
дълбок [dulbok] *adj.* deep
дълбоко [dulboko] *adv.* deeply
дълбочина [dulbochina] *n.* depth
дълг [dulg] *n.* debt
дължина [dulzhina] *n.* length
дълъг [dulug] *adj.* long
дума [duma] n. word
дървени въглища [durveni vuglishta] *n. pl.* charcoal
дърво [durvo] *n.* tree
държа [durzha] *v.* keep, hold
дърпам [durpam] *v.* pull
дъска [duska] *n.* board

Е

евтин [evtin] *adj.* cheap
едва [edva] *adv.* hardly
един [edin] *num.* one
единичен [edinichen] *adj.* single
еднакъв [ednakuv] *adj.* equal
едно време [edno vreme] *adv.* once (in the past)
ежегоден [ezhegoden] *adj.* annual
ежедневен [ezhedneven] *adj.* daily
език [ezik] *n.* tongue; language
екстра [ekstra] *adj.* extra
еластичен [elastichen] *adj.* elastic
елегантен [eleganten] *adj.* elegant
електричество [elektrichestvo] *n.* electricity
електроника [elektronika] *n.* electronics
електронна поща [elektronna poshta] *n.* e-mail

елементарен [elementaren] *adj.* simple, basic
еленско месо [elensko meso] *n.* venison
емисия [emisiya] *n.* emission
енергия [energiya] *n.* energy
ера [era] *n.* era
ерген [ergen] *n.* bachelor (unmarried man)
есен [esen] *n.* autumn, fall
етажерка за книги [etazherka za knigi] *n.* bookcase

Ж

жажда [zhazhda] *n.* thirst
желая [zhelaya] *v.* wish
железница [zheleznitsa] *n.* railroad
жена [zhena] *n.* female, woman
женски [zhenski] *adj.* female
жесток [zhestok] *adj.* cruel
жив [zhiv] *adj.* alive
живея [zhiveya] *v.* live
живот [zhivot] *n.* life
животно [zhivotno] *n.* animal
жизнен [zhiznen] *adj.* vital
жилище [zhilishte] *n.* apartment, flat, residence
жител [zhitel] *n.* resident
жълт [zhult] *adj.* yellow
жълтък [zhultuk] *n.* yolk

З

за [za] *prep.* for, about
за жалост [za zhalost] *adv.* unfortunately
забавление [zabavlenie] *n.* entertainment
забождам [zabozhdam] *v.* stick

забравям [zabravyam] *v.* forget
забрана [zabrana] *n.* ban
забранявам [zabranyavam] *v.* forbid
завивам [zavivam] *v.* wrap; turn
завивки [zavivki] *n. pl.* bedclothes
завинаги [zavinagi] *adv.* forever
завися [zavisya] *v.* depend
завой [zavoy] *n.* bend, curve
загуба [zagouba] *n.* loss
зад [zad] *prep.* behind
задна седалка [zadna sedalka] *n.* back seat
задължавам се [zadulzhavam se] *v.* engage, oblige oneself
задължение [zadulzhenie] *n.* obligation, duty
заедно [zaedno] *adv.* together
заек [zaek] *n.* rabbit
заем [zaem] *n.* loan
заинтересуван [zainteresouvan] *adj.* interested
закачвам [zakachvam] *v.* hang
заключвам [zaklyuchvam] *v.* lock
закон [zakon] *n.* law
закуска [zakouska] *n.* breakfast
закъснение [zakusnenie] *n.* delay
залез [zalez] *n.* sunset
залог [zalog] *n.* bail
заминаване [zaminavane] *n.* departure
замък [zamuk] *n.* castle
запад [zapad] *n.* west
запалянко [zapalyanko] *n.* fan
запис [zapis] *n.* record
записвам [zapisvam] *v.* record, write down
заплата [zaplata] *n.* pay, wage
заповядвам [zapovyadvam] *v.* command

започвам [zapochvam] *v.* start, begin
засрамен [zasramen] *adj.* ashamed
застраховка [zastrahovka] *n.* insurance
затварям [zatvaryam] *v.* shut
затвор [zatvor] *n.* prison
захар [zahar] *n.* sugar
защита [zashtita] *n.* protection
защо [zashto] *adv.* why
защото [zashtoto] *conj.* because
звезда [zvezda] *n.* star
звънец [zvunets] *n.* bell
здраве [zdrave] *n.* health
здравей [zdravey] *interj.* hello
зелен [zelen] *adj.* green
зеленчук [zelenchouk] *n.* vegetable
земя [zemya] *n.* land, ground, earth
зима [zima] *n.* winter
злато [zlato] *n.* gold
знаме [zname] *n.* flag
знание [znanie] *n.* knowledge
значение [znachenie] *n.* matter; meaning
зная [znaya] *v.* know
зодиак [zodiak] *n.* zodiac
зоологическа градина [zoologicheska gradina] *n.* zoo
зрение [zrenie] *n.* vision
зъб [zub] *n.* tooth
зъбен [zuben] *adj.* dental
зъболекар [zubolekar] *n.* dentist
зърнена храна [zurnena hrana] *n.* cereal

И

и [i] *conj.* and
игла [igla] *n.* needle
игра [igra] *n.* game, play
играчка [igrachka] *n.* toy

играя [igraya] *v.* play
идвам [idvam] *v.* come
идентифицирам [identifitsiram] *v.* identify
идея [ideya] *n.* idea
изход [izhod] *n.* exit
избирам [izbiram] *v.* pick, choose
избор [izbor] *n.* choice
известен [izvesten] *adj.* famous
извънреден труд [izvunreden troud] *n.* overtime
изглед [izgled] *n.* view, landscape; aspect
изглеждам [izglezhdam] *v.* seem
изгода [izgoda] *n.* profit, advantage
изгрев [izgrev] *n.* sunrise
издавам [izdavam] *v.* publish
издание [izdanie] *n.* publication, issue, edition
изделие [izdelie] *n.* article, product
изисквам [iziskvam] *v.* require
изключение [izklyuchenie] *n.* exception
изкуство [izkoustvo] *n.* art
излизам [izlizam] *v.* issue
изложба [izlozhba] *n.* display, exhibition
изложение [izlozhenie] *n.* statement; exhibition, fair
измислям [izmislyam] *v.* fabricate
изморен [izmoren] *adj.* tired
изненада [iznenada] *n.* surprise
използвам [izpolzvam] *v.* apply, use
изпращам [izprashtam] *v.* send
изпускам [izpouskam] *v.* miss, omit, drop down
изпълнявам [izpulnyavam] *v.* perform
изследвам [izsledvam] *v.* investigate

изследване [izsledvane] *n.* research, investigation, examination
изток [iztok] *n.* east
изчезвам [izchezvam] *v.* disappear
изчисление [izchislenie] *n.* calculation
или [ili] *conj.* or
илюстрирам [ilyustriram] *v.* illustrate
имам [imam] *v.* have
име [ime] *n.* name
имитирам [imitiram] *v.* imitate
иначе [inache] *adv.* otherwise
инвестиция [investitsiya] *n.* investment
индекс [indeks] *n.* index
индивид [individ] *n.* individual
индустриален [indoustrialen] *adj.* industrial
индустрия [industriya] *n.* industry
инициатива [initsiativa] *n.* initiative
институт [institout] *n.* institute
институция [institoutsiya] *n.* institution
инструмент [instroument] *n.* instrument
интервю [intervyu] *n.* interview
интерес [interes] *n.* interest
интересен [interesen] *adj.* interesting
инфлация [inflatsiya] *n.* inflation
информация [informatsiya] *n.* information
информирам [informiram] *v.* inform
инцидент [intsident] *n.* accident
искам [iskam] *v.* want
искане [iskane] *n.* demand
истина [istina] *n.* truth
истински [istinski] *adj.* real
исторически [istoricheski] *adj.* historic
история [istoriya] *n.* story; history

К

кавга [kavga] *n.* quarrel
кадърност [kadurnost] *n.* skillfulness, ability
казвам [kazvam] *v.* tell, say
кайсия [kaysiya] *n.* apricot
как [kak] *adv.* how
какао [kakao] *n.* cocoa
какво [kakvo] *pron.* what
както и да [kakto i da] *adv.* however
какъв [kakuv] *pron.* what
календар [kalendar] *n.* calendar
канела [kanela] *n.* cinnamon
кантар [kantar] *n.* balance, scales
канцелария [kantselariya] *n.* office
каня [kanya] *v.* invite
капак [kapak] *n.* cover
капка [kapka] *n.* drop
капки за очи [kapki za ochi] *n. pl.* eye-drops
карамфил [karamfil] *n.* carnation
карта [karta] *n.* map; card
картина [kartina] *n.* picture
картичка [kartichka] *n.* postcard
картон [karton] *n.* cardboard
картонена кутия [kartonena koutiya] *n.* carton
картоф [kartof] *n.* potato
карфиол [karfiol] *n.* cauliflower
каса [kasa] *n.* ticket office
касиер [kasier] *n.* cashier
катастрофа [katastrofa] *n.* accident, crash
катедра [katedra] *n.* desk
катеря се [katerya se] *v.* climb
катинар [katinar] *n.* padlock

като [kato] *prep.* like
като [kato] *adv.* as
католически [katolicheski] *adj.* Catholic
кафе [kafe] *n.* coffee
кафяв [kafyav] *adj.* brown
кацам [katsam] *v.* land
качество [kachestvo] *n.* quality
кашлица [kashlitsa] *n.* cough
кекс [keks] *n.* cake
кибрит [kibrit] *n.* match, box of matches
кино [kino] *n.* cinema
киселина [kiselina] *n.* acid
клас [klas] *n.* category
клиника [klinika] *n.* clinic
клон [klon] *n.* branch
клюкарствам [klyukarstvam] *v.* backbite
ключ [klyuch] *n.* key
ключалка [klyuchalka] *n.* lock
книга [kniga] *n.* book
книговезец [knigovezets] *n.* binder
кога [koga] *adv.* when
когато [kogato] *conj.* as
кожа [kozha] *n.* skin
кой [koy] *pron.* which; who
кой да е [koy da e] *adj.* either
който [koyto] *pron.* which
кокосов орех [kokosov oreh] *n.* coconut
кола [kola] *n.* vehicle, car, carriage
колело [kolelo] *n.* bicycle
коленича [kolenicha] *v.* kneel
количество [kolichestvo] *n.* quantity
коляно [kolyano] *n.* knee
комин [komin] *n.* chimney
компания [kompaniya] *n.* company
компютър [kompyutur] *n.* computer
кон [kon] *n.* horse

конец [konets] *n.* thread
контрола [kontrola] *n.* check
конфитюр [konfityur] *n.* jam
концерт [kontsert] *n.* concert
копая [kopaya] *v.* dig
копие [kopie] *n.* copy
копче [kopche] *n.* button
кораб [korab] *n.* ship
корав [korav] *adj.* hard
кораво [koravo] *adv.* hard
корен [koren] *n.* root
коридор [koridor] *n.* corridor
коса [kosa] *n.* hair
костюм [kostyum] *n.* suit
котка [kotka] *n.* cat
котлет [kotlet] *n.* cutlet
кофа [kofa] *n.* bucket
краен срок [kraen srok] *n.* deadline
краен [kraen] *adj.* final
край [kray] *n.* end, finish; *prep.* by
крайно [krayno] *adv.* extremely, excessively
крак [krak] *n.* leg, foot
крал [kral] *n.* king
красив [krasiv] *adj.* beautiful
краставица [krastavitsa] *n.* cucumber
кратък [kratuk] *adj.* short
крачка [krachka] *n.* step
края на седмицата [kraya na sedmit-sata] *n.* weekend
кредит [kredit] *n.* credit
кредитор [kreditor] *n.* creditor
крикет [kriket] *n.* cricket
кристал [kristal] *n.* crystal
критичен [kritichen] *adj.* critical
крия [kriya] *v.* hide
крокет [kroket] *n.* croquet

кръв [kruv] *n.* blood
кръг [krug] *n.* circle
кръст [krust] *n.* waist
кръчма [kruchma] *n.* pub
кукла [koukla] *n.* doll
кула [koula] *n.* tower
културен [koultouren] *adj.* cultural
купувам [koupouvam] *v.* buy
курабийка [kourabiyka] *n.* cookie
кутия [koutiya] *n.* box
куфар [koufar] *n.* suitcase
кухня [kouhnya] *n.* kitchen
куче [kouche] *n.* dog
къде [kude] *adv.* where
към [kum] *prep.* into, towards
къпя се [kupya se] *v.* bathe
кървя [kurvya] *v.* bleed
къри [kuri] *n.* curry
кърпа за ръце [kurpa za rutse] *n.* hand towel
куршум [kourshoum] *n.* bullet
късам [kusam] *v.* tear
късен [kusen] *adj.* late
къща [kushta] *n.* home, house

Л

лагер [lager] *n.* camp
лампа [lampa] *n.* lamp
легло [leglo] *n.* bed
лед [led] *n.* ice
лежа [lezha] *v.* lie
лекар [lekar] *n.* physician, doctor
лекарство [lekarstvo] *n.* drug, medicine
лекувам [lekouvam] *v.* treat, heal
лента [lenta] *n.* tape
лепило [lepilo] *n.* glue

лесен [lesen] *adj.* easy
летище [letishte] *n.* airport
летя [letya] *v.* fly
лечение [lechenie] *n.* treatment, cure
лешник [leshnik] *n.* hazelnut
лимон [limon] *n.* lemon
линейка [lineyka] *n.* ambulance
линия [liniya] *n.* line
липса [lipsa] *n.* lack
лист [list] *n.* leaf
лице [litse] *n.* face
личен [lichen] *adj.* personal
лодка [lodka] *n.* boat
лош [losh] *adj.* bad
лошо [losho] *adv.* badly
лук [louk] *n.* onion
лъв [luv] *n.* lion
лъжица [luzhitsa] *n.* spoon
любимец [lyubimets] *n.* darling, favorite
любов [lyubov] *n.* love
лютив [lyutiv] *adj.* hot, spicy
лято [lyato] *n.* summer

M

магазин [magazin] *n.* shop, store
мазе [maze] *n.* basement
мазен [mazen] *adj.* greasy, fat
май [may] *n.* May
майка [mayka] *n.* mother
макар че [makar che] *conj.* although
малко [malko] *adv.* few, little
малцинство [maltsinstvo] *n.* minority
малък [maluk] *adj.* small
манипулирам [manipouliram] *v.* manipulate, handle

марка [marka] *n.* stamp; brand, trademark
март [mart] *n.* March
маса [masa] *n.* table
масло [maslo] *n.* butter
мастило [mastilo] *n.* ink
материал [material] *n.* fabric, material; matter
машина [mashina] *n.* machine
машинно масло [mashinno maslo] *n.* machine oil
мед [med] *n.* honey
медицинска сестра [meditsinska sestra] *n.* nurse
медицински [meditsinski] *adj.* medical
между [mezhdou] *prep.* among, between
междувременно [mezhdouvremenno] *adv.* meanwhile
международен [mezhdounaroden] *adj.* international
мек [mek] *adj.* soft
меля [melya] *v.* grind
мен [men] *pron.* me
месец [mesets] *n.* month
месо [meso] *n.* meat
местен [mesten] *adj.* local
местоимение [mestoimenie] *n. gram.* pronoun
метален чайник [metalen chaynik] *n.* kettle
метод [metod] *n.* method
метро [metro] *n.* subway
механик [mehanik] *n.* mechanic
мивка [mivka] *n.* basin, sink, washbowl
мил [mil] *adj.* dear
мина [mina] *n.* mine

минавам [minavam] *v.* pass
минал [minal] *adj.* past
минало [minalo] *n.* past
минута [minouta] *n.* minute
мир [mir] *n.* peace
мириша [mirisha] *v.* smell
мисля [mislya] *v.* think, contemplate
мисъл [misul] *n.* idea, thought
млад [mlad] *adj.* young
млад лук [mlad luk] *n.* chives
младост [mladost] *n.* youth
млекарница [mlekarnitsa] *n.* dairy
мляко [mlyako] *n.* milk
мнение [mnenie] *n.* opinion
много [mnogo] *adv.* much, very; *adj.* many
множествено число [mnozhestveno chislo] *n. gram.* plural form
мога [moga] *v.* can, may
мода [moda] *n.* trend, fashion
модерен [moderen] *adj.* modern, fashionable
може би [mozhe bi] *adv.* perhaps, maybe
мокър [mokur] *adj.* wet
молба [molba] *n.* application, appeal
молив [moliv] *n.* pencil
моля [molya] *interj.* please
мома [moma] *n.* maid, maiden
момент [moment] *n.* while
момиче [momiche] *n.* girl
момче [momche] *n.* guy, boy
монета [moneta] *n.* coin
море [more] *n.* sea
морков [morkov] *n.* carrot
мост [most] *n.* bridge
мотор [motor] *n.* motor; motorcycle

мразя [mrazya] *v.* hate
мрежа [mrezha] *n.* network
мръсен [mrusen] *adj.* dirty
мръсотия [mrusotiya] *n.* dirt
музей [mouzey] *n.* museum
музика [mouzika] *n.* music
мъгла [mugla] *n.* fog
мъж [muzh] *n.* man
мъжки [muzhki] *adj.* male
мярка [myarka] *n.* measure
място [myasto] *n.* place, space

Н

на [na] *prep.* at; on
на глас [na glas] *adv.* aloud
на здраве [na zdrave] *interj.* cheers
на палубата [na palubata] *adv.* aboard
набелязвям си [nabelyazvam si] *v.* note
наблизо [nablizo] *prep.* near; *adj.* close
наблюдавам [nablyudavam] *v.* watch, observe
наблюдение [nablyudenie] *n.* observation
навечерие [navecherie] *n.* eve
навсякъде [navsyakude] *adv.* anywhere
навън [navun] *adv.* outside
навярно [navyarno] *adv.* probably
нагоре [nagore] *adv.* up
награда [nagrada] *n.* award
над [nad] *prep.* over, above
надежда [nadezhda] *n.* hope
надявам се [nadyavam se] *v.* hope
наем [naem] *n.* rent
назначавам [naznachavam] *v.* appoint
назовавам [nazovavam] *v.* name
най-малък [nai-maluk] *adj.* least
наистина [naistina] *adv.* indeed

най-много [nay-mnogo] *adv.* most
най-хубав [nay-hubav] *adj.* best
налагам [nalagam] *v.* impose
наляво [nalyavo] *adv.* to/on the left
налягане [nalyagane] *n.* pressure
намаление [namalenie] *n.* discount
намалявам [namalyavam] *v.* reduce
намерение [namerenie] *n.* intention, aim
намигане [namigane] *n.* blink
намирам [namiram] *v.* find
наново [nanovo] *adv.* anew
наоколо [naokolo] *adv.* around
нападам [napadam] *v.* attack
нападениае [napadenie] *n.* attack
напитка [napitka] *n.* drink
направо [napravo] *adv.* right ahead, directly
напред [napred] *adv.* forward, ahead
напредък [napreduk] *n.* advance, progress
напълно [napulno] *adv.* completely
напускам [napuskam] *v.* abandon
нареждам [narezhdam] *v.* order
нареждане [narezhdane] *n.* arrangement, order
наречие [narechie] *n. gram.* adverb
народен [naroden] *adj.* national
насекомо [nasekomo] *n.* insect
настанявам се [nastanyavam se] *v.* settle
настаняване [nastanyavane] *n.* accommodations
настинка [nastinka] *n.* cold
настоявам [nastoyavam] *v.* insist
настройка [nastroyka] *n.* attitude
наука [naouka] *n.* science
начален [nachalen] *adj.* initial

началник [nachalnik] *n.* manager, boss
начин [nachin] *n.* way
не [ne] *part.* no, not
не съм съгласен [ne sum suglasen] *v.* disagree
небе [nebe] *n.* sky
невъзможен [nevuzmozhen] *adj.* impossible
негативен [negativen] *adj.* negative
негов [negov] *pron.* his
недалеко [nedaleko] *adv.* nearby
неделя [nedelya] *n.* Sunday
недостатък [nedostatuk] *n.* defect
независим [nezavisim] *adj.* independent
независимост [nezavisimost] *n.* independence
необикновен [neobiknoven] *adj.* extraordinary, unusual
необходим [neobhodim] *adj.* necessary
неотдавна [neotdavna] *adv.* recently
неотложен [neotlozhen] *adj.* urgent
непознат [nepoznat] *adj.* unknown
непосредствен [neposredstven] *adj.* immediate
неспособен [nesposoben] *adj.* unable
нещо [neshto] *n.* thing; *pron.* anything
нея [neya] *pron.* her
неин [nein] *pron.* her
ниво [nivo] *n.* level
ние [nie] *pron.* we
никакъв [nikakuv] *pron.* no, none
никога [nikoga] *adv.* never
никой [nikoy] *pron.* nobody, none
ниско [nisko] *adv.* low
нисък [nisuk] *adj.* low, short
нито единия(т), нито другия(т) [nito ediniya(t) nito drougiya(t)] *pron.* neither

нищо [nishto] *pron.* nothing
но [no] *conj.* but
нов [nov] *adj.* new
новина [novina] *n.* news
ноември [noemvri] *n.* November
нож [nozh] *n.* knife
ножица [nozhitsa] *n.* scissors
нокът [nokut] *n.* nail
нормален [normalen] *adj.* normal
нос [nos] *n.* nose
носна кърпа [nosna kurpa] *n.* handkerchief
нося [nosya] *v.* wear; carry
нощ [nosht] *n.* night
нужда [nouzhda] *n.* need
нуждая се [nouzhdaya se] *v.* need
нула [noula] *n.* zero
някакъв [nyakakuv] *adj.* some
някой [nyakoy] *pron.* anybody
няколко [nyakolko] *adj.* several
някъде [nyakude] *adv.* somewhere

О

обаче [obache] *adv.* however
обвинение [obvinenie] *n.* blame
обвинявам [obvinyavam] *v.* accuse
обграждам [obgrazhdam] *v.* enclose, surround
обещавам [obeshtavam] *v.* promise
обикновен [obiknoven] *adj.* ordinary, usual
обикновено [obiknoveno] *adv.* usually, generally
обица [obitsa] *n.* earring
обичам [obicham] *v.* love
облак [oblak] *n.* cloud

област [oblast] *n.* region
облекло [obleklo] *n.* clothing, apparel
обмяна [obmayana] *n.* exchange
обозначавам [oboznachavam] *v.* designate
образ [obraz] *n.* image
образец [obrazets] *n.* model, pattern, sample
образовам [obrazovam] *v.* educate
образование [obrazovanie] *n.* education
обратен [obraten] *adj.* backward
обръщам се [obrushtam se] *v.* turn about/around; appeal
обръщам внимание [obrushtam vni-manie] *v.* pay attention, mind
обръщане [obrushtane] *n.* turn
обсег [obseg] *n.* range
обсъждам [obsuzhdam] *v.* argue, discuss
обсъждане [obsuzhdane] *n.* debate
обувка [obouvka] *n.* shoe
обучавам [obouchavam] *v.* teach
обучение [obouchenie] *n.* instruction
обширен [obshiren] *adj.* vast
общежитие [obshtezhitie] *n.* dormitory
обществен [obshtestven] *adj.* social
обявявам [obyavyavam] *v.* announce
обяд [obyad] *n.* lunch, dinner
обядвам [obyadvam] *v.* have lunch, dine
обяснение [obyasnenie] *n.* explanation, interpretation
обяснявам [obyasnyavam] *v.* explain, interpret
овесена каша [ovesena kasha] *n.* porridge
огледало [ogledalo] *n.* mirror
ограда [ograda] *n.* fence
огромен [ogromen] *adj.* huge

огън [ogun] *n.* fire
одеяло [odeyalo] *n.* blanket
одобрявам [odobryavam] *v.* approve
оженвам се [ozhenvam se] *v.* marry (*for a male*)
означавам [oznachavam] *v.* mark
око [oko] *n.* eye
октомври [oktomvri] *n.* October
окуражавам [okourazhavam] *v.* encourage
олио [olio] *n.* oil
опаковам [opakovam] *v.* pack
опаковка [opakovka] *n.* wrapper
опасност [opasnost] *n.* danger
опит [opit] *n.* attempt
опитвам [opitvam] *v.* try
оплаквам се [oplakvam se] *v.* complain
оправям [opravyam] *v.* fix
определям [opredelyam] *v.* determine
опция [optsiya] *n.* option
оранжев [oranzhev] *adj.* orange
организация [organizatsiya] *n.* organization
организирам [organiziram] *v.* organize
орех [oreh] *n.* walnut
ориз [oriz] *n.* rice
оса [osa] *n.* wasp
осведомявам [osvedomyavam] *v.* inform
освежаване [osvezhavane] *n.* refreshment
освен [osven] *prep.* except
освен това [osven tova] *adv.* besides
осезание [osezanie] *n.* sense (of touch), feeling
осем [osem] *num.* eight
основа [osnova] *n.* foundation
основен [osnoven] *adj.* fundamental, basic
оставам [ostavam] *v.* stay

оставям [ostavyam] *v.* leave
остров [ostrov] *n.* island
осъзнавам [osuznavam] *v.* realize
осъществявам се [osushtestvyavam se] *v.* proceed
от [ot] *prep.* off, from; **(от-)** *adv.* off
отбягвам [otbyagvam] *v.* avoid
отварям [otvaryam] *v.* open
отвор [otvor] *n.* opening
отворен [otvoren] *adj.* open
отвращение [otvrashtenie] *n.* disgust
отговарям [otgovaryam] *v.* reply, respond, answer
отговарям (за нещо) [otgovaryam (za neshto)] *v.* account (for)
отговор [otgovor] *n.* response, answer
отгоре [otgore] *adv.* above
отделен [otdelen] *adj.* separate
отделно [otdelno] *adv.* separately, apart
отдолу [otdolou] *adv.* below
отивам [otivam] *v.* go
отказвам [otkazvam] *v.* refuse
отключвам [otklyuchvam] *v.* unlock
откривам [otkrivam] *v.* discover
откъде [otkude] *adv.* from where, where
отличен [otlichen] *adj.* excellent
отменям [otmenyam] *v.* cancel
отново [otnovo] *adv.* anew, again
отпред [otpred] *adv.* at the front, ahead
отричам [otricham] *v.* deny
отхвърлям [othvurlyam] *v.* reject
оценявам [otsenyavam] *v.* assess, evaluate
оценявям [otsenyavyam] *v.* appreciate
оцет [otset] *n.* vinegar
отсъствие [otsustvie] *n.* absence
очаквам [ochakvam] *v.* expect
очевиден [ocheviden] *adj.* apparent

очевидно [ochevidno] *adv.* apparently
още [oshte] *adv.* yet
още веднъж [oshte vednuzh] *adv.* once again

П

падам [padam] *v.* fall
падане [padane] *n.* fall
пазар [pazar] *n.* market
пазарувам [pazarouvam] *v.* buy
пазаруване [pazarouvane] *n.* shopping
пазя [pazya] *v.* protect
пакет [paket] *n.* packet, package
палачинка [palachinka] *n.* pancake
палто [palto] *n.* coat
памук [pamouk] *n.* cotton
панталон [pantalon] *n.* trousers
панталони [pantaloni] *n. pl.* pants
пардон [pardon] *interj.* sorry
пари [pari] *n.* money, cash
парк [park] *n.* park
паркинг [parking] *n.* parking
паркирам [parkiram] *v.* park
парламент [parlament] *n.* parliament
партия [partiya] *n.* party
партньор [partnyor] *n.* partner
парче [parche] *n.* piece, bit, cut
пасаж [pasazh] *n.* passage
пасвам [pasvam] *v.* fit
паспорт [pasport] *n.* passport
паста за зъби [pasta za zubi] *n.* toothpaste
пациент [patsient] *n.* patient
певец [pevets] *n.* singer
пека [peka] *v.* bake
пека на скара [peka na skara] *v.* grill

пека се (на слънце) [peka se (na sluntse)] *v.* bask
пекарница [pekarnitsa] *n.* bakery
пелена [pelena] *n.* diaper
пеперуда [peperuda] *n.* butterfly
пера [pera] *v.* wash, do the laundry
пералня [peralnya] *n.* washing machine
перде [perde] *n.* curtain
период [period] *n.* term, period
песен [pesen] *n.* song
пет [pet] *num.* five
петно [petno] *n.* spot
петък [petuk] *n.* Friday
печалба [pechalba] *n.* profit, prize
печеля [pechelya] *v.* gain, win
печка [pechka] *n.* stove
пещера [peshtera] *n.* cave
пея [peya] *v.* sing
пиене [piene] *n.* drinking
пиле [pile] *n.* chicken
писалище [pisalishte] *n.* writing table, desk
писалка [pisalka] *n.* pen
писане [pisane] *n.* writing
писател [pisatel] *n.* writer
писмо [pismo] *n.* letter
питам [pitam] *v.* question, ask
питие [pitie] *n.* drink, beverage
пиша [pisha] *v.* write
пия [piya] *v.* drink
пиян [piyan] *adj.* drunk
пладне [pladne] *n.* noon, midday
плаж [plazh] *n.* beach
план [plan] *n.* plan
планина [planina] *n.* mountain
планирам [planiram] *v.* plan
плач [plach] *n.* cry

плащам [plashtam] *v.* pay
плащане [plashtane] *n.* payment
пленявам [plenyavam] *v.* capture
плета [pleta] *v.* knit
плик [plik] *n.* envelope
плод [plod] *n.* fruit
площ [plosht] *n.* area
площад [ploshtad] *n.* square
плувам [plouvam] *v.* swim
плът [plut] *n.* flesh
пляскам [plyaskam] *v.* clap
по [po] *prep.* along
по продължение на [po produlzhenie na] *adv.* along
по време на [po vreme na] *prep.* during
победа [pobeda] *n.* victory
повече [poveche] *adv.* more
повикване [povikvane] *n.* call
повишавам [povishavam] *v.* promote
повреда [povreda] *n.* damage
повръщам [povrushtam] *v.* vomit
повтарям [povtaryam] *v.* repeat
поглед [pogled] *n.* look
под [pod] *prep.* under; *n.* floor
подарък [podaruk] *n.* present, gift
подготвям [podgotvyam] *v.* prepare
подготовка [podgotovka] *n.* preparation
подир [podir] *adv.* after
подкрепа [podkrepa] *n.* aid, assistance
подлог [podlog] *n. gram.* subject
подобен [podoben] *adj.* similar, alike
подобно [podobno] *adv.* similarly
подобрение [podobrenie] *n.* improvement
подобрявам [podobryavam] *v.* improve
подправка [podpravka] *n.* spice
подразбирам [podrazbiram] *v.* imply

подредба [podredba] *n.* arrangement
подреждам [podrezhdam] *v.* arrange
подслонявам [podslonyavam] *v.* house
подход [podhod] *n.* approach
подходящ [podhodyasht] *adj.* suitable, appropriate
поза [poza] *n.* attitude
позволявам [pozvolyavam] *v.* allow
позволявам си [pozvolyavam si] *v.* afford
поздрав [pozdrav] *n.* greeting
поздравявам [pozdravyavam] *v.* congratulate
познание [poznanie] *n.* cognition
показвам [pokazvam] *v.* show
покрив [pokriv] *n.* roof
по-късен [po-kusen] *adj.* later, latter
покъщнина [pokushtnina] *n.* household goods/belongings
поле [pole] *n.* field
полезен [polezen] *adj.* useful
полет [polet] *n.* flight
полза [polza] *n.* use, advantage
полицай [politsay] *n.* policeman
полиция [politsiya] *n.* police
половина [polovina] *n.* half
положение [polozhenie] *n.* position
получавам [polouchavam] *v.* get, receive, obtain
помагам [pomagam] *v.* help
по-малко [po-malko] *adv.* less
помощ [pomosht] *n.* aid, assistance, help
по-нататък [po-natatuk] *adv.* farther
понеделник [ponedelnik] *n.* Monday
поправка [popravka] *n.* repair
поражение [porazhenie] *n.* defeat

портмоне [portmone] *n.* wallet
портокал [portokal] *n.* orange
порцелан [portselan] *n.* china
поръчвам [poruchvam] *v.* order
поръчка [poruchka] *n.* order
порязвам се [poryazvam se] *v.* cut
порязване [poryazvane] *n.* cut
посвещавам [posveshtavam] *v.* devote
посещавам [poseshtavam] *v.* visit
посещение [poseshtenie] *n.* visit
по-скоро [po-skoro] *adv.* rather
после [posle] *adv.* afterwards
последен [posleden] *adj.* last
посочвам [posochvam] *v.* indicate
поставям [postavyam] *v.* place, lay
постигам [postigam] *v.* achieve, acquire
постижение [postizhenie] *n.* achievement
постоянен [postoyanen] *adj.* permanent
постройка [postroyka] *n.* construction
построявам [postroyavam] *v.* build
потвърден [potvurden] *adj.* confirmed
потвърждавам [potvurzhdavam] *v.* certify
поток [potok] *n.* stream, flow
похвала [pohvala] *n.* praise
почва [pochva] *n.* soil
почивка [pochivka] *n.* rest
почти [pochti] *adv.* almost
поща [poshta] *n.* mail, post
правдив [pravdiv] *adj.* true
правилен [pravilen] *adj.* correct
правило [pravilo] *n.* rule
правителство [pravitelstvo] *n.* government
правя [pravya] *v.* do; make
правя възможно [pravya vuzmozhno] *v.* make possible, facilitate

празен [prazen] *adj.* empty
празник [praznik] *n.* holiday; feast
празничен [praznichen] *adj.* festive
празнувам [praznouvam] *v.* celebrate
праскова [praskova] *n.* peach
прах [prah] *n.* dust, ash, powder
превключвател [prevklyuchvatel] *n.* switch
предположение [pregpolozhenie] *n.* assumption
пред [pred] *prep.* in front of, before
преден [preden] *adj.* front
преди [predi] *adv.* ago
преди обед [predi obed] *n.* a.m.
преди пладне [predi pladne] *n.* a.m.
предишен [predishen] *adj.* prior
предишно [predishno] *adv.* previously
предлагам [predlagam] *v.* offer
предлог [predlog] *n. gram.* preposition
предложение [predlozhenie] *n.* proposal, offer
предмет [predmet] *n.* object, article
предпазлив [predpazliv] *adj.* wary, cautious
предполагам [predpolagam] *v.* suppose, assume
предпочитам [predpochitam] *v.* prefer
представление [predstavlenie] *n.* performance
представям [predstavyam] *v.* present
представям си [predstavyam si] *v.* imagine
предупреждавам [predouprezhdavam] *v.* warn
през [prez] *prep.* through, via, across
презиме [prezime] *n.* surname
прекрасен [prekrasen] *adj.* wonderful
прекъсвам [prekusvam] *v.* interrupt

премествам [premestvam] *v.* shift
препечена филийка [prepechena filiyka] *n.* toast
препоръчвам [preporuchvam] *v.* recommend
преса [presa] *n.* press
пресен [presen] *adj.* fresh
преследвам [presledvam] *v.* pursue
преставам [prestavam] *v.* cease
претеглям [preteglyam] *v.* weigh
преча [precha] *v.* be an obstacle; disturb
преча на [precha na] *v.* prevent
прешлен [preshlen] *n.* vertebra
при [pri] *prep.* by, at
при това [pri tova] *adv.* also
прибавям [pribavyam] *v.* add
приближаване [priblizhavane] *n.* approaching
приветствам [privetstvam] *v.* welcome
привечер [privecher] *n.* dusk
привлекателен [privlekatelen] *adj.* attractive
придобивам [pridobivam] *v.* acquire
придружавам [pridruzhavam] *v.* accompany
прием [priem] *n.* party
приемам [priemam] *v.* admit, accept
признавам [priznavam] *v.* acknowledge, admit
прикрепвам [prikrepvam] *v.* attach
прилагателно [prilagatelno] *n. gram.* adjective
пример [primer] *n.* example
принадлежа [prinadlezha] *v.* belong
приоритет [prioritet] *n.* priority
природа [priroda] *n.* nature
природен [priroden] *adj.* natural

пристанище [pristanishte] *n.* port
пристигам [pristigam] *v.* arrive
присъстващ [prisustvasht] *adj.* present
присъствие [prisustvie] *n.* presence
притежавам [pritezhavam] *v.* own
прицелвам се [pritselvam se] *v.* aim
причина [prichina] *n.* reason, cause
приятел [priyatel] *n.* friend
приятелски [priyatelski] *adj.* friendly
приятелство [priyatelstvo] *n.* friendship, fellowship
провалям се [provalyam se] *v.* fail
провеждам [provezhdam] *v.* conduct, carry out
провизии [provizii] *n. pl.* provision
продавам [prodavam] *v.* sell
продажба [prodazhba] *n.* sale
продукт [prodoukt] *n.* product
продължавам [produlzhavam] *v.* proceed, continue, last
проект [proekt] *n.* project
проектант [proektant] *n.* designer
проза [proza] *n.* fiction
прозорец [prozorets] *n.* window
произвеждам [proizvezhdam] *v.* fabricate
произшествие [proizshestvie] *n.* accident, incident
пролет [prolet] *n.* spring
промеждутък [promezhdoutuk] *n.* gap
променада [promenada] *n.* esplanade
променям [promenyam] *v.* alter
проповядвам [propovyadvam] *v.* preach
прост [prost] *adj.* simple
против [protiv] *prep.* against
професионалист [profesionalist] *n.* expert

професия [profesiya] *n.* profession
процес [protses] *n.* process
прощавам [proshtavam] *v.* forgive
пристигане [prstigane] *n.* arrival
пръст [prust] *n.* finger
пръст на крак [prust na krak] *n.* toe
пръстен [prusten] *n.* ring
пръчка [pruchka] *n.* bar
пряк [pryak] *adj.* direct
птица [ptitsa] *n.* bird
публика [poublika] *n.* audience
публичен [poublichen] *adj.* public
пуловер [poulover] *n.* sweater
пура [poura] *n.* cigar
пуша [pousha] *v.* smoke
пчела [pchela] *n.* bee
пълно [pulno] *adv.* fully
пълня [pulnya] *v.* fill
първи [purvi] *adj.* first
първичен [purvichen] *adj.* primary
първоначален [purvonachalen] *adj.* original
пържа [purzha] *v.* fry
пърхут [purhout] *n.* dandruff
път [put] *n.* road, route, drive
пътека [puteka] *n.* path
пътник [putnik] *n.* passenger
пътувам [putouvam] *v.* travel
пътуване [putouvane] *n.* journey, trip, travel
пяна [pyana] *n.* foam

Р

работа [rabota] *n.* employment, work, job, affair
работник [rabotnik] *n.* worker
работя [rabotya] *v.* work
равен [raven] *adj.* even, level
радвам се [radvam se] *v.* enjoy
радост [radost] *n.* joy
раждане [razhdane] *n.* birth
разбирам [razbiram] *v.* understand
развивам [razvivam] *v.* develop
развод [razvod] *n.* divorce
разговор [razgovor] *n.* talk
раздяла [razdyala] *n.* separation
разкошен [razkoshen] *adj.* magnificent, luxurious, lovely
разлика [razlika] *n.* difference
различавам се [razlichavam se] *v.* differ
различен [razlichen] *adj.* different, alternative
размер [razmer] *n.* size
разнообразие [raznoobrazie] *n.* variety
разочаровам [razocharovam] *v.* disappoint
разпилявам [razpilyavam] *v.* scatter, disperse
разписка [razpiska] *n.* receipt
разпознавам [razpoznavam] *v.* recognize
разрешавам [razreshavam] *v.* allow, let, permit
разрешение [razreshenie] *n.* permit
разстояние [razstoyanie] *n.* distance
разтварям [raztvaryam] *v.* dissolve
разтопявам [raztopyavam] *v.* melt, thaw, dissolve
разум [razoum] *n.* mind, sense

разумен [razoumen] *adj.* reasonable, sensible
рамка [ramka] *n.* frame
рамо [ramo] *n.* shoulder
рана [rana] *n.* injury, wound
раста [rasta] *v.* grow
растеж [rastezh] *n.* growth, increase
растение [rastenie] *n.* plant
ревност [revnost] *n.* jealousy
революция [revolyutsiya] *n.* revolution
ред [red] *n.* order, system; row, line
редица [reditsa] *n.* row, line; *pl.* series
редовен [redoven] *adj.* regular
резултат [rezoultat] *n.* outcome
река [reka] *n.* river
религия [religiya] *n.* religion
рентгенов лъч [rengenov luch] *n.* X-ray
република [repoublika] *n.* republic
ресторант [restorant] *n.* restaurant, café
рецепта [retsepta] *n.* prescription; recipe
реч [rech] *n.* speech
речник [rechnik] *n.* dictionary
решавам [reshavam] *v.* decide
решение [reshenie] *n.* solution
риба [riba] *n.* fish
рикоширам [rikoshiram] *v.* ricochet, glance (off)
рисувам [risouvam] *v.* draw, paint
рисунка [risounka] *n.* drawing, painting
ритник [ritnik] *n.* kick
роден [roden] *adj.* born
родител [roditel] *n.* parent
рожден ден [rozhden den] *n.* birthday
розов [rozov] *adj.* pink
рокля [roklya] *n.* dress
роса [rosa] *n.* dew
ръб [rub] *n.* edge

ръка [ruka] *n.* hand, arm
ръкавица [rukavitsa] *n.* glove
ръководител [rukovoditel] *n.* leader
ръководя [rukovodya] *v.* manage
рядък [ryaduk] *adj.* rare

С

с (със) [s (sus)] *prep.* with
сако [sako] *n.* coat, jacket
салон [salon] *n.* hall
сам [sam] *adj.* alone
самка [samka] *n.* female (animal)
само [samo] *adv.* only
самолет [samolet] *n.* plane, aircraft, airplane
самоличност [samolichnost] *n.* identity
сапун [sapoun] *n.* soap
сблъсквам се [sbluskvam se] *v.* collide
сбогуване [sbogouvane] *n.* farewell
сбор [sbor] *n.* sum, total
сборник [sbornik] *n.* collection, digest
сватба [svatba] *n.* wedding, marriage
сведение [svedenie] *n.* (a piece of) information
светвам [svetvam] *v.* light
светлина [svetlina] *n.* light
световъртеж [svetovurtezh] *n.* vertigo
свиждане [svizdane] *n.* appointment, visit
свинско месо [svinsko meso] *n.* pork
свобода [svoboda] *n.* freedom
свободен [svoboden] *adj.* free
свой [svoy] *adj.* your, own
свръзка [svruzka] *n.* tie, link
свързвам [svurzvam] *v.* bind
свят [svyat] *n.* world

сгоден [sgoden] *adj.* engaged
сгодявам се [sgodyavam se] *v.* get engaged
сделка [sdelka] *n.* bargain, deal
сдружение [sdrouzhenie] *n.* association
север [sever] *n.* north
сега [sega] *adv.* now
седем [sedem] *num.* seven
седмица [sedmitsa] *n.* week
седя [sedya] *v.* sit
сезон [sezon] *n.* season
секретарка [sekretarka] *n.* secretary
село [selo] *n.* village
селски [selski] *adj.* rural
семейство [semeystvo] *n.* family
септември [septemvri] *n.* September
сервитьор [servityor] *n.* waiter
сериозен [seriozen] *adj.* serious
сертификат [sertifikat] *n.* certificate
сестра [sestra] *n.* sister
сив [siv] *adj.* gray
сигурен [sigouren] *adj.* safe, certain, sure
сила [sila] *n.* power, force
силен [silen] *adj.* strong
син [sin] *adj.* blue; *n.* son
сирене [sirene] *n.* cheese
сироп [sirop] *n.* syrup
сит [sit] *adj.* full
скала [skala] *n.* scale
скамейка [skameyka] *n.* bench
скара [skara] *n.* barbecue
скачам [skacham] *v.* jump
скоро [skoro] *adv.* soon
скъп [skup] *adj.* dear, beloved; expensive, costly
слаб [slab] *adj.* weak, faint

слава [slava] *n.* fame
слагам [slagam] *v.* put, apply
сладкарница [sladkarnitsa] *n.* confectionary
сладък [sladuk] *adj.* sweet
сланина [slanina] *n.* bacon; fat
след [sled] *adv.* after
след обед [sled obed] *n.* p.m.
следвам [sledvam] *v.* follow
следващ [sledvasht] *adj.* further, next, following
следобед [sledobed] *n.* afternoon
следствие [sledstvie] *n.* consequence; inquiry, investigation
слива [sliva] *n.* plum
слизане [slizane] *n.* descent
слуга [slouga] *n.* servant
служба [slouzhba] *n.* service
служебен [slouzheben] *adj.* official
случай [slouchay] *n.* case, occasion
случва се [slouchva se] *v.* happen
случка [slouchka] *n.* incident, event
слушам [slousham] *v.* listen; obey
слънце [sluntse] *n.* sun
сменям [smenyam] *v.* barter
смесвам [smesvam] *v.* mix
сметана [smetana] *n.* cream
сметка [smetka] *n.* bill, account
смешен [smeshen] *adj.* funny
смея се [smeya se] *v.* laugh
смущавам [smoushtavam] *v.* disturb
смяна [smyana] *n.* exchange, change
собствен [sobstven] *adj.* proper
собственик [sobstvenik] *n.* owner
сол [sol] *n.* salt
сос [sos] *n.* sauce, gravy
спалня [spalnya] *n.* bedroom

спанак [spanak] *n.* spinach
спасявам [spasyavam] *v.* save
специфичен [spetsifichen] *adj.* particular, specific
спирам [spiram] *v.* stop
спирка [spirka] *n.* stop
списание [spisanie] *n.* magazine
списък [spisuk] *n.* list
споменавам [spomenavam] *v.* mention
спомням си [spomnyam si] *v.* remember
спор [spor] *n.* dispute
споразумение [sporazoumenie] *n.* agreement, understanding, deal
според [spored] *prep.* according
способен [sposoben] *adj.* able
справедлив [spravedliv] *adj.* fair
справедливост [spravedlivost] *n.* justice
справка [spravka] *n.* reference
спускам се [spouskam se] *v.* descend
спя [spya] *v.* sleep
сравнявам [sravnyavam] *v.* compare
среда [sreda] *n.* center
среден [sreden] *adj.* middle
среща [sreshta] *n.* appointment, date
срещам [sreshtam] *v.* meet
срещу [sreshtou] *prep.* against
сряда [sryada] *n.* Wednesday
става [stava] *n.* joint
ставам [stavam] *v.* become; get up
стандарт [standart] *n.* standard
станция [stantsiya] *n.* station
стар [star] *adj.* old
статия [statiya] *n.* article
стафида [stafida] *n.* raisin
стая [staya] *n.* chamber, room
стая в хотел [staya v hotel] *n.* hotel room

стена [stena] *n.* wall
степен [stepen] *n.* degree
стига [stiga] *adv.* enough
стипендия [stipendiya] *n.* scholarship, grant
стол [stol] *n.* seat, chair; cafeteria
столетие [stoletie] *n.* century
столица [stolitsa] *n.* capital
стоя [stoya] *v.* stand
стража [strazha] *n.* guard
страна [strana] *n.* country; side
страница [stranitsa] *n.* page
страхувам се [strahouvam se] *v.* (be) afraid
строя [stroya] *v.* build
стряха [stryaha] *n.* eaves, roof
студ [stoud] *n.* cold
стъкло [stuklo] *n.* glass
стълба [stulba] *n.* ladder
сума [souma] *n.* amount
супа [soupa] *n.* soup
супермаркет [soupermarket] *n.* supermarket
суров [sourov] *adj.* raw
сутрин [soutrin] *n.* morning
сух [souh] *adj.* dry
суша [sousha] *n.* drought
сцена [stsena] *n.* stage, scene
считам [schitam] *v.* consider, regard
събирам [subiram] *v.* collect, gather
събиране [subirane] *n.* meeting
събота [subota] *n.* Saturday
събрание [subranie] *n.* assembly
събуждам се [subouzhdam se] *v.* wake up, awake
съвет [suvet] *n.* advice
съветвам [suvetvam] *v.* advise

съвсем [suvsem] *adv.* quite
съвършен [suvurshen] *adj.* perfect
съгласие [suglasie] *n.* assent, agreement
съгласявам се [suglasyavam se] *v.* agree
съглашение [suglashenie] *n.* agreement, alliance
съдия [sudiya] *n.* judge
съдържам [sudurzham] *v.* contain
съдя [sudya] *v.* judge
съединявам [suedinyavam] *v.* unite, associate, join, combine
сълза [sulza] *n.* tear (from eye)
съм [sum] *v.* be
сън [sun] *n.* dream
съобщение [suobshtenie] *n.* message, notice
съпротива [suprotiva] *n.* resistance, opposition
съпруг [suproug] *n.* husband
съпруга [suprouga] *n.* wife
сърдит [surdit] *adj.* angry
сърце [surtse] *n.* heart
със сигурност [sus sigournost] *adv.* definitely
съсед [sused] *n.* neighbor
състезание [sustezanie] *n.* race
състояние [sustoyanie] *n.* state
същ [susht] *adj.* equal, same
съществително [sushtestvitelno] *n.* *gram.* noun
също [sushto] *adv.* also
съюз [suyuz] *n.* union, alliance; *gram.* conjunction
сянка [syanka] *n.* shadow

Т

таблетка [tabletka] *n.* pill
таван [tavan] *n.* ceiling
така [taka] *adv.* so
такса [taksa] *n.* fee
такси [taksi] *n.* cab, taxi
такъв [takuv] *adj.* such
там [tam] *adv.* there
танц [tants] *n.* dance
танцувална зала [tantsouvalna zala] *n.* ballroom
твой [tvoy] *pron.* yours; *adj.* your
твърд [tvurd] *adj.* hard, firm
твърдо [tvurdo] *adv.* hard
те [te] *pron.* they
театър [teatur] *n.* theater
тебешир [tebeshir] *n.* chalk
тегло [teglo] *n.* weight
тежко [tezhko] *adv.* heavily
тежък [tezhuk] *adj.* heavy
телефон [telefon] *n.* phone, telephone
телешко месо [teleshko meso] *n.* veal
температура [temperatoura] *n.* temperature
тесен [tesen] *adj.* narrow
ти [ti] *pron.* you
тиган [tigan] *n.* pan
тиква [tikva] *n.* pumpkin
тих [tih] *adj.* quiet
тичане [tichane] *n.* run
то [to] *pron.* it
тоалетна [toaletna] *n.* bathroom, toilet
тоалетна хартия [toaletna hartiya] *n.* toilet paper
тогава [togava] *adv.* then
той [toy] *pron.* he

топка [topka] *n.* ball
топлина [toplina] *n.* heat
топъл [topul] *adj.* warm
торба [torba] *n.* sack
точка [tochka] *n.* item, point
точно [tochno] *adv.* precisely, exactly, just
традиция [traditsiya] *n.* tradition
трамвай [tramvay] *n.* tram, streetcar
транспорт [transport] *n.* transport
трафик [trafik] *n.* traffic
трева [treva] *n.* grass
треска [treska] *n.* fever
три [tri] *num.* three
труд [troud] *n.* labor
труден [trouden] *adj.* difficult
тръгвам [trugvam] *v.* start, embark (on), depart
тръгвам на път [trugvam na put] *v.* embark
тръпчив [trupchiv] *adj.* bitter
трябва [tryabva] *v.* must
тук [touk] *adv.* here
тур [tour] *n.* tour
тухла [touhla] *n.* brick
тъкан [tukan] *n.* texture
тъмен [tumen] *adj.* dark
тънък [tunuk] *adj.* thin
търговия [turgoviya] *n.* trade
търся [tursya] *v.* seek, search
тютюн [tyutyun] *n.* tobacco
тя [tya] *pron.* she
тяло [tyalo] *n.* body
тях [tyah] *pron.* them

У

убивам [oubivam] *v.* kill
уважавам [ouvazham] *v.* respect, honor
уважение [ouvazhenie] *n.* respect
увеличавам [ouvelichavam] *v.* increase
увеличаващ се [ouvelichavasht se] *adj.* increasing
уверен [ouveren] *adj.* confident, certain
уверявам [ouveryavam] *v.* assure
увод [ouvod] *n.* introduction, preface
угощение [ougoshtenie] *n.* feast
удар [oudar] *n.* hit, impact
удоволствие [oudovolstvie] *n.* pleasure
удостоявам [oudostoyavam] *v.* dignify
удрям [oudryam] *v.* knock, hit
украсявам [oukrasyavam] *v.* decorate
улица [oulitsa] *n.* street
ум [oum] *n.* mind, intellect
умен [oumen] *adj.* clever
умение [oumenie] *n.* skill, ability
умея [oumeya] *v.* can, know (how)
умора [oumora] *n.* fatigue
университет [ouniversitet] *n.* college, university
унижавам [ounizhavam] *v.* abase, humiliate
унищожавам [ounishtozhavam] *v.* destroy
употребявам [oupotrebyavam] *v.* use
управление [oupravlenie] *n.* administration, management
урина [ourina] *n.* urine
урок [ourok] *n.* lesson
усмивка [ousmivka] *n.* smile
успех [ouspeh] *n.* success
успешен [ouspeshen] *adj.* successful

успявам [ouspyavam] *v.* succeed
уста [ousta] *n.* mouth
устна [oustna] *n.* lip
утре [outre] *adv.* tomorrow
ухо [ouho] *n.* ear
уча [oucha] *v.* study
уча се [oucha se] *v.* learn
училище [ouchilishte] *n.* school
учител [ouchitel] *n.* teacher

Ф

фабрика [fabrika] *n.* factory
факт [fakt] *n.* fact
фактура [faktoura] *n.* invoice
февруари [fevrouari] *n.* February
ферма [ferma] *n.* farm
фермер [fermer] *n.* farmer
фигура [figoura] *n.* figure
филм [film] *n.* film
финанси [finansi] *n.* finance
финансии [finansii] *n.* banking
фирма [firma] *n.* company, firm
фокусирам [fokousiram] *v.* focus
фонд [fond] *n.* fund
форма [forma] *n.* form
формален [formalen] *adj.* formal
формация [formatsiya] *n.* formation
формирам [formiram] *v.* form
форсирам [forsiram] *v.* force
фотоапарат [fotoaparat] *n.* camera
фотография [fotografiya] *n.* photograph
фронт [front] *n.* front
функция [founktsiya] *n.* function
фурна [fourna] *n.* oven, bakery
фурнаджия [fournadzhiya] *n.* baker

футбол [foutbol] *n.* soccer
фъстък [fustuk] *n.* peanut

Х

хайвер [hayver] *n.* caviar
харесвам [haresvam] *v.* like
хартия [hartiya] *n.* paper
харча [harcha] *v.* spend
хваля се [hvalya se] *v.* brag
хващам [hvashtam] *v.* catch
хвърлям [hvurlyam] *v.* throw
хит [hit] *n.* fad; blockbuster
хлад [hlad] *n.* chill
хладен [hladen] *adj.* cool
хладилник [hladilnik] *n.* refrigerator
хляб [hlyab] *n.* bread
ходя [hodya] *v.* walk
хора [hora] *n. pl.* folk, people
хотел [hotel] *n.* hotel
храна [hrana] *n.* food, nourishment
хубав [houbav] *adj.* nice, fine, pretty
художник [houdozhnik] *n.* artist
хълм [hulm] *n.* hill

Ц

цар [tsar] *n.* king
царевица [tsarevitsa] *n.* corn
царица [tsaritsa] *n.* queen
царски [tsarski] *adj.* royal
цвете [tsvete] *n.* flower
цвят [tsvyat] *n.* color; blossom
цел [tsel] *n.* aim, goal
целина [tselina] *n.* celery
целувка [tselouvka] *n.* kiss
целя [tselya] *v.* aim

цена [tsena] *n.* price, cost
ценност [tsennost] *n.* value
цент [tsent] *n.* cent
централен [tsentralen] *adj.* central
церемония [tseremoniya] *n.* ceremony
цигара [tsigara] *n.* cigarette
цимент [tsiment] *n.* cement
цитирам [tsitiram] *v.* quote
цял [tsyal] *adj.* whole, entire
цялостен [tsyalosten] *adj.* complete, integral, total

Ч

чадър [chadur] *n.* umbrella
чай [chay] *n.* tea
чакам [chakam] *v.* wait, await
чанта [chanta] *n.* handbag, bag
чар [char] *n.* charm
час [chas] *n.* appointment; hour
часовник [chasovnik] *n.* watch, clock
част [chast] *n.* part
частица [chastitsa] *n. gram.* particle
частично [chastichno] *adv.* partly
чаша [chasha] *n.* cup, glass
чело [chelo] *n.* forehead
червен [cherven] *adj.* red
черен [cheren] *adj.* black
черен дроб [cheren drob] *n.* liver
череша [cheresha] *n.* cherry
черква [cherkva] *n.* church
често [chesto] *adv.* frequently, often
чесън [chesun] *n.* garlic
чета [cheta] *v.* read
четвъртина [chetvurtina] *n.* quarter
четвъртък [chetvurtuk] *n.* Thursday
четири [chetiri] *num.* four

четка [chetka] *n.* brush
четка за зъби [chetka za zubi] *n.* toothbrush
Чехия [Chehiya] *n.* Czech Republic
чешки [cheshki] *adj.* Czech, Bohemian
чиния [chiniya] *n.* plate, dish
чиновник [chinovnik] *n.* official
числително [chislitelno] *n. gram.* numeral
число [chislo] *n.* number
чист [chist] *adj.* clean
чистене [chistene] *n.* cleaning
чифт [chift] *n.* pair
член [chlen] *n.* member
членство [chlenstvo] *n.* membership
човек [chovek] *n.* person; man, guy
човек на изкуството [chovek na izkoustvoto] *n.* artist
човешки [choveshki] *adj.* human
чувам [chouvam] *v.* hear
чувство [chouvstvo] *n.* feeling
чужд [chouzhd] *adj.* foreign
чукам [choukam] *v.* knock
чукване [choukvane] *n.* knock
чупя [choupya] *v.* break

Ш

шампанско [shampansko] *n.* champagne
шанс [shans] *n.* chance
шапка [shapka] *n.* hat, cap
шах [shah] *n.* chess
шест [shest] *num.* six
шеф [shef] *n.* boss, chief
широк [shirok] *adj.* wide
шоколад [shokolad] *n.* chocolate
шофьор [shofyor] *n.* driver, chauffeur

шум [shoum] *n.* noise
шунка [shounka] *n.* ham

Щ

щастлив [shtastliv] *adj.* lucky; happy
що [shto] *pron.* what
щурец [shturets] *n.* cricket

Ъ

ъгъл [ugul] *n.* angle

Ю

юг [yug] *n.* south
юли [yuli] *n.* July
юни [yuni] *n.* June

Я

ябълка [yabulka] *n.* apple
явен [yaven] *adj.* obvious
ядене [yadene] *n.* meal
ядосан [yadosan] *adj.* angry
ядрен [yadren] *adj.* nuclear
язовир [yazovir] *n.* dam
яйце [yaytse] *n.* egg
яка [yaka] *n.* collar
ям [yam] *v.* eat
януари [yanouari] *n.* January

ENGLISH–BULGARIAN DICTIONARY

A

abandon *v.* напускам [napuskam]
abase *v.* унижавам [ounizhavam]
ability *n.* умение [oumenie], кадърност [kadurnost]
able *adj.* способен [sposoben]
aboard *adv.* на палубата [na palubata]
about *prep.* за [za]
above *adv.* отгоре [otgore]
absence *n.* отсъствие [otsustvie]
absolutely *adv.* абсолютно [absolyutno]
academic *adj.* академически [akademicheski]
accept *v.* приемам [priemam]
access *n.* достъп [dostup]
accident *n.* катастрофа [katastrofa], инцидент [intsident]
accommodations *n.* настаняване [nastanyavane]
accompany *v.* придружавам [pridruzhavam]
according *prep.* според [spored]
account *n.* сметка [smetka]
account (for) *v.* отговарям (за нещо) [otgovaryam (za neshto)]
accuse *v.* обвинявам [obvinyavam]
achieve *v.* постигам [postigam]
achievement *n.* постижение [postizhenie]
acid *n.* киселина [kiselina]
acknowledge *v.* признавам [priznavam]
acquire *v.* придобивам [pridobivam], постигам [postigam]
across *prep.* през [prez]
act *n.* акт [akt], действие [deystvie]; *v.* действам [deystvam]

action *n.* действие [deystvie], акция [aktsiya]
active *adj.* активен [aktiven]
activity *n.* активност [aktivnost]
actual *adj.* действителен [deystvitelen]
actually *adv.* всъщност [vsushnost]
add *v.* прибавям [pribavyam]
addition *n.* допълнение [dopulnenie], добавка [dobavka]
additional *adj.* допълнителен [dopulnitelen]
address *n.* адрес [adres]
adjective *n. gram.* прилагателно [prilagatelno]
administration *n.* администрация [administratsiya], управление [oupravlenie]
admire *v.* възхищавам се [vuzhishtavam se]
admit *v.* признавам [priznavam], приемам [priemam]
adopt *v.* осиновявам [osinovyavam]
adult *adj.* възрастен [vuzrasten]; *n.* възрастен [vuzrasten]
advance *n.* напредък [napreduk]
advantage *n.* полза [polza], изгода [izgoda], предимство [predimstvo]
adverb *n. gram.* наречие [narechie]
advice *n.* съвет [suvet]
advise *v.* съветвам [suvetvam]
affair *n.* работа [rabota], въпрос [vupros]
affect *v.* въздействам [vuzdeystvam]
afford *v.* позволявам си [pozvolyavam si]
afraid *v.* страхувам се [strahouvam se]
after *adv.* след [sled]
afternoon *n.* следобед [sledobed]

afterwards *adv.* след това [sled tova], после [posle]
again *adv.* отново [otnovo],
against *prep.* срещу [sreshtou], против [protiv]
age *n.* възраст [vuzrast]
agency *n.* бюро [byuro], агенция [agentsiya]
agenda *n.* дневен ред [dneven red]
agent *n.* деятел [deyatel]
ago *adv.* преди [predi]
agree *v.* съгласявам се [suglasyavam se]
agreement *n.* съгласие [suglasie], договор [dogovor]
ahead *adv.* отпред [otpred]; напред [napred]
aid *n.* помощ [pomosht], подкрепа [podkrepa]
aim *v.* прицелвам се [pritselvam se]; целя [tselya]; *n.* намерение [namere-nie]; цел [tsel]
air *n.* въздух [vuzdouh]
aircraft *n.* самолет [samolet]
airplane *n.* самолет [samolet]
airport *n.* летище [letishte]
alike *adj.* подобен [podoben]
alive *adj.* жив [zhiv]
all *adj.* всичко [vsichko]
alliance *n.* съглашение [suglashenie], съюз [suyuz]
allow *v.* позволявам [pozvolyavam], разрешавам [razreshavam]
almost *adv.* почти [pochti]
alone *adj.* сам [sam]
along *adv.* по продължение на [po produlzhenie na]; *prep.* по [po]
aloud *adv.* на глас [na glas]

alphabet *n.* азбука [azbouka]
already *adv.* вече [veche]
also *adv.* също [sushto], при това [pri tova]
alter *v.* променям [promenyam]
alternative *adj.* алтернативен [alternativen], различен [razlichen]
although *conj.* макар че [makar che]; въпреки че [vupreki che]
always *adv.* винаги [vinagi]
a.m. *n.* преди обед [predi obed], преди пладне [predi pladne]
ambulance *n.* линейка [lineyka], бърза помощ [burza pomosht]
American *adj.* американски [amerikanski]; *n.* американец [amerikanets]
among *prep.* между [mezhdou]
amount *n.* сума [souma], сбор [sbor]
analysis *n.* анализ [analiz]
analyze *v.* анализирам [analiziram], правя анализ [pravya analiz]
ancient *adj.* древен [dreven]
and *conj.* и [i], а [a]
anew *adv.* отново [otnovo], наново [nanovo]
angle *n.* ъгъл [ugul]
angry *adj.* сърдит [surdit], ядосан [yadosan]
animal *n.* животно [zhivotno]
announce *v.* анонсирам [anonsiram], обявявам [obyavyavam]
annual *adj.* годишен [godishen]; ежегоден [ezhegoden]
another *adj.* допълнителен [dopulnitelen], още един [oshte edin]
answer *n.* отговор [otgovor]; *v.* отговарям [otgovaryam]

any *adj.* всякакъв [vsyakakuv]
anybody *pron.* някой [nyakoy]
anything *pron.* нещо [neshto]
anywhere *adv.* навсякъде [navsyakude]
apart *adv.* отделено [otdelno]
apartment *n.* апартамент [apartament], жилище [zhilishte]
apparent *adj.* очевиден [ocheviden]
apparently *adv.* очевидно [ochevidno]
appeal *n.* молба [molba], апел [apel]; *v.* апелирам [apeliram], обръщам се [obrushtam se]
apple *n.* ябълка [yabulka]
application *n.* молба [molba]
apply *v.* използвам [izpolzvam], слагам [slagam]
appoint *v.* назначавам [naznachavam]
appointment *n.* среща [sreshta]; свиждане [svizdane], час [chas]
appreciate *v.* оценявям [otsenyavyam], ценя [tsenya]
approach *n.* приближаване [priblizha-vane], подход [podhod]
appropriate *adj.* подходящ [podhodyasht]
approve *v.* одобрявам [odobryavam]
apricot *n.* кайсия [kaysiya]
April *n.* април [april]
area *n.* площ [plosht]
argue *v.* обсъждам [obsuzhdam]
argument *n.* довод [dovod]
arm *n.* ръка [ruka]
army *n.* армия [armiya], войска [voyska]
around *adv.* около, наоколо [naokolo]
arrange *v.* аранжирам [aranzhiram], подреждам [podrezhdam]
arrangement *n.* нареждане [narezdane], подредба [podredba]

arrival *n.* пристигане [prstigane]
arrive *v.* пристигам [pristigam]
art *n.* изкуство [izkoustvo]
article *n.* вид [vid], предмет [predmet]; статия [statiya], изделие [izdelie]
artist *n.* художник [houdozhnik], човек на изкуството [chovek na izkoustvoto]
as *adv.* като [kato]; *conj.* когато [kogato]
ash *n.* прах [prah]
ashamed *adj.* засрамен [zasramen]
ask *v.* питам [pitam]
aspect *n.* изглед [izgled], аспект [aspekt]
aspiration *n.* амбиция [ambitsiya]
assembly *n.* събрание [subranie]
assent *n.* съгласие [suglasie]
assess *v.* оценявам [otsenyavam]
assets *n.* актив [aktiv]
assistance *n.* помощ [pomosht], подкрепа [podkrepa]
associate *v.* съединявам [suedinyavam]
association *n.* асоциация [asotsiatsiya], сдружение [sdrouzhenie]
assume *v.* предполагам [predpolagam]
assumption *n.* предположение [pregpolozhenie]
assure *v.* уверявам [ouveryavam]
at *prep.* в [v], на [na], при [pri]
at all *adv.* въобще [vuobshte]
atmosphere *n.* атмосфера [atmosfera]
attach *v.* прикрепвам [prikrepvam]
attack *n.* атака [ataka], нападениае [napadenie]; *v.* нападам [napadam]
attempt *n.* опит [opit]
attention *n.* внимание [vnimanie]
attitude *n.* поза [poza]; настройка [nastroyka]
attractive *adj.* атрактивен [atraktiven],

привлекателен [privlekatelen]
audience *n.* публика [poublika]
August *n.* август [avgust]
author *n.* автор [avtor]
authority *n.* власт [vlast]
autumn *n.* есен [esen]
available *adj.* достъпен [dostupen]
avoid *v.* отбягвам [otbyagvam]
await *v.* чакам [chakam]
awake *v.* събуждам се [subouzhdam se]
award *n.* награда [nagrada]
away *adv.* далеч [dalech]

B

baby *n.* бебе [bebe]
bachelor *n.* ерген [ergen]
back *n.* гръб [grub]
backbite *v.* клюкарствам [klyukarstvam]
backbone *n.* гръбначен стълб [grub-nachen stulb]
backseat *n.* задна седалка [zadna sedalka]
backward *adj.* обратен [obraten]
bacon *n.* сланина [slanina]
bacteria *n.* бактерия [bakteriya]
bad *adj.* лош [losh]
badly *adv.* лошо [losho]
bag *n.* чанта [chanta]
bail *n.* залог [zalog]
bake *v.* пека [peka]
baker *n.* фурнаджия [fournadzhiya]
bakery *n.* фурна [fourna], пекарница [pekarnitsa]
balance *n.* кантар [kantar]
balcony *n.* балкон [balkon]
baldly *adv.* направо [napravo]

ball *n.* топка [topka]
ballroom *n.* танцувална зала [tantsouvalna zala]
ban *n.* забрана [zabrana]
banal *adj.* банален [banalen]
banana *n.* банан [banan]
bangle *n.* гривна [grivna]
bank *n.* банка [banka]
banking *n.* финансии [finansii]
banknote *n.* банкнота [banknota]
banquet *n.* банкет [banket]
bar *n.* пръчка [pruchka]
barbecue *n.* скара [skara]
barber *n.* бръснар [brusnar]
bargain *n.* сделка [sdelka]
baroque *adj.* бароков [barokov]
barter *v.* сменям [smenyam]
basement *n.* мазе [maze], сутерен [suteren]
basic *adj.* основен [osnoven], елементарен [elementaren]
basically *adv.* в основата си [v osnovata si]
basin *n.* мивка [mivka]
bask *v.* пека се (на слънце) [peka se (na sluntse)]
basketball *n.* баскетбол [basketbol]
bath *n.* баня [banya]
bathe *v.* къпя се [kupya se]
bathroom *n.* баня [banya], тоалетна [toaletna]
bathtub *n.* вана [vana]
be *v.* съм [sum]
beach *n.* плаж [plazh]
bean *n.* боб [bob]
beard *n.* брада [brada]
beautiful *adj.* красив [krasiv]

because *conj.* защото [zashtoto]
become *v.* ставам [stavam]
bed *n.* легло [leglo]
bedclothes *n. pl.* завивки [zavivki]
bedroom *n.* спалня [spalnya]
bee *n.* пчела [pchela]
beef *n.* говеждо месо [govezhdo meso]
beer *n.* бира [bira]
before *prep.* пред [pred], преди [predi]
begin *v.* започвам [zapochvam]
behalf (on ~ of) *n.* от името на [ot imeto na], заради [zaradi]
behind *prep.* зад [zad]
bell *n.* звънец [zvunets]
belong *v.* принадлежа [prinadlezha]
beloved *adj.* любим [lyubim], скъп [skup]
below *adv.* отдолу [otdolou], ниско [nisko]
bench *n.* пейка [peyka], скамейка [skameyka]
bend *n.* завой [zavoy]
besides *adv.* освен това [osven tova]
best *adj.* най-хубав [nay-hubav]
between *prep.* между [mezhdou]
beverage *n.* питие [pitie]
bicycle *n.* колело [kolelo]
big *adj.* голям [golyam]
bill *n.* сметка [smetka]; банкнота [banknote]
billiards *n.* билярд [bilyard]
bind *v.* свързвам [svurzvam], връзвам [vruzvam]
binder *n.* книговезец [knigovezets]
binoculars *n.* бинокъл [binokul]
biography *n.* биография [biografiya]
bird *n.* птица [ptitsa]

birth *n.* раждане [razhdane]
birthday *n.* рожден ден [rozhden den]
biscuit *n.* бисквита [biskvita],
bit *n.* парче [parche]
bitter *adj.* горчив [gorchiv], тръпчив [trupchiv]
black *adj.* черен [cheren]
blame *n.* вина [vina], обвинение [obvinenie]
blanket *n.* одеяло [odeyalo]
bleed *v.* кървя [kurvya]
blink *n.* намигане [namigane]
blood *n.* кръв [kruv]
bloom *n.* цвят [tsvyat]
blouse *n.* блуза [blouza]
blue *adj.* син [sin]
board *n.* дъска [duska]
boat *n.* лодка [lodka]
body *n.* тяло [tyalo]
boil *v.* варя [varya]
boiling *adj.* врял [vryal]
book *n.* книга [kniga]
bookcase *n.* библиотека [biblioteka], етажерка за книги [etazherka za knigi]
border *n.* граница [granitsa]
born *adj.* роден [roden]
bottle *n.* бутилка [boutilka]
bouquet *n.* букет [bouket]
box *n.* кутия [koutiya]
boy *n.* момче [momche]
bracelet *n.* гривна [grivna]
brag *v.* хваля се [hvalya se]
branch *n.* клон [klon]
bread *n.* хляб [hlyab]
break *v.* чупя [choupya]
breakfast *n.* закуска [zakouska]
breast *n.* бюст [byust]

breath *n.* дишане [dishane]
brick *n.* тухла [touhla]
bridge *n.* мост [most]
bring *v.* донасям [donasyam]
brother *n.* брат [brat]
brown *adj.* кафяв [kafyav]
brush *n.* четка [chetka]
bucket *n.* кофа [kofa]
build *v.* строя [stroya], построявам [postroyavam]
Bulgaria *n.* България [Bulgariya]
Bulgarian *adj.* български [bulgarski]
bullet *n.* куршум [kourshoum]
bus *n.* автобус [avtobous]
business *n.* бизнес [biznes]
but *conj.* но [no]
butter *n.* масло [maslo]
butterfly *n.* пеперуда [peperouda]
button *n.* копче [kopche]
buy *v.* купувам [koupouvam], пазарувам [pazarouvam]
by *prep.* при [pri], край [kray]; близо[blizo]; чрез [chrez]
bye *interj.* довиждане [dovizhdane], чао [chao]

C

cab *n.* такси [taksi]
café *n.* кафене [kafene], кафе-сладкарница [kafe-sladkarnitsa], ресторант [restorant]
cafeteria *n.* стол [stol], ресторант на самообслужване [restorant na samoobsluzhvane]
cake *n.* кекс [keks]
calculation *n.* изчисление [izchislenie]

calendar *n.* календар [kalendar]
call *n.* повикване [povikvane]; *v.* викам [vikam]
camera *n.* фотоапарат [fotoaparat]
camp *n.* лагер [lager]
can *v.* мога [moga]; умея [oumeya]
cancel *v.* отменям [otmenyam]
candy *n.* бонбон [bonbon]
cap *n.* шапка [shapka]
capital *n.* столица [stolitsa]
captain *n.*капитан [kapitan]
capture *v.* пленявам [plenyavam]
car *n.* автомобил [avtomobil], кола [kola]
card *n.* картон [karton]
care *n.* грижа [grizha]; *v.* грижа се [grizha se]
carnation *n.* карамфил [karamfil]
carriage *n.* кола [kola]
carrot *n.* морков [morkov]
carry *v.* нося [nosya]
carton *n.* картонена кутия [kartonena koutiya]
case *n.* случай [slouchay]
cash *n.* пари в брой [pari v broy]
cashier *n.* касиер [kasier]
castle *n.* замък [zamuk]
cat *n.* котка [kotka]
catch *v.* хващам [hvashtam]
category *n.* категория [kategoriya], клас [klas]
Catholic *adj.* католически [katolicheski]; *n.* католик [katolik]
cauliflower *n.* карфиол [karfiol]
cause *n.* причина [prichina]
cautious *adj.* внимателен [vnimatelen], предпазлив [predpazliv]

cave *n.* пещера [peshtera]
caviar *n.* хайвер [hayver]
cease *v.* преставам [prestavam]
ceiling *n.* таван [tavan]
celebrate *v.* празнувам [praznouvam]
celery *n.* целина [tselina]
cement *n.* цимент [tsiment]
cent *n.* цент [tsent]
center *n.* център [tsentur], среда [sreda]
central *adj.* централен [tsentralen]
century *n.* столетие [stoletie]
cereal *n.* зърнена храна [zurnena hrana]
ceremony *n.* церемония [tseremoniya]
certain *adj.* сигурен [sigouren], уверен [ouveren]
certificate *n.* сертификат [sertifikat]
certify *v.* потвърждавам [potvurzhdavam]
chain *n.* верижка [verizhka]
chair *n.* стол [stol]
chalk *n.* тебешир [tebeshir]
chamber *n.* стая [staya]
champagne *n.* шампанско [shampansko]
chance *n.* шанс [shans], възможност [vuzmozhnost]
change *n.* смяна [smyana]
chapter *n.* глава [glava]
charcoal *n. pl.* дървени въглища [dur-veni vuglishta]
charm *n.* чар [char]
chauffeur *n* .(личен) шофьор [(lichen) shofyor]
cheap *adj.* евтин [evtin]
check *n.* контрола [kontrola]
cheek *n.* буза [bouza]
cheers! *interj.* на здраве [na zdrave]
cheese *n.* сирене [sirene]
cherry *n.* череша [cheresha]

chess *n.* шах [shah]
chew *v.* дъвча [duvcha]
chicken *n.* пиле [pile]
chief *n.* шеф [shef], началник [nachalnik]
child *n.* дете [dete]
chill *n.* хлад [hlad]
chimney *n.* комин [komin]
chin *n.* брада [brada], брадичка [bradichka]
china *n.* порцелан [portselan]
chives *n.* млад лук [mlad luk]
chocolate *n.* шоколад [shokolad]
choice *n.* избор [izbor]
choose *v.* избирам [izbiram]
church *n.* черква [cherkva]
cigar *n.* пура [poura]
cigarette *n.* цигара [tsigara]
cinema *n.* кино [kino]
cinnamon *n.* канела [kanela]
circle *n.* кръг [krug]
citizen *n.* гражданин [grazhdanin]
city *n.* град [grad]
clap *v.* пляскам [plyaskam]
clean *adj.* чист [chist]
cleaning *n.* чистене [chistene]
clear *adj.* бистър [bistur]
clever *adj.* умен [oumen]
climb *v.* катеря се [katerya se]
clinic *n.* клиника [klinika]
clock *n.* часовник [chasovnik]
close *adj.* наблизо [nablizo]
clothes *n.* дрехи [drehi], облекло [obleklo]
cloud *n.* облак [oblak]
coal *n. pl.* въглища [vuglishta]
coat *n.* палто [palto]
cocoa *n.* какао [kakao]
coconut *n.* кокосов орех [kokosov oreh]
coffee *n.* кафе [kafe]

cognition *n.* познание [poznanie]
coin *n.* монета [moneta]
cold *n.* студ [stoud]; настинка [nastinka]
collar *n.* яка [yaka]
collect *v.* събирам [subiram]
college *n.* университет [ouniversitet]
collide *v.* сблъсквам се [sbluskvam se]
color *n.* цвят [tsvyat]
comb *n.* гребен [greben]
combine *v.* съединявам [suedinyavam]
come *v.* идвам [idvam]
come in *v.* влизам [vlizam]
command *v.* заповядвам [zapovyadvam]; ръководя [rukovodya]
company *n.* компания [kompaniya]
compare *v.* сравнявам [sravnyavam]
complain *v.* оплаквам се [oplakvam se]
completely *adv.* напълно [napulno]
computer *n.* компютър [kompyutur]
concern *n.* грижа [grizha]
concert *n.* концерт [kontsert]
confectionery *n.* сладкарница [sladkar-nitsa]
confirmed *adj.* потвърден [potvurden]
congratulate *v.* поздравявам [poz-dravyavam]
conjunction *n. gram.* съюз [suyuz]
construction *n.* постройка [postroyka]
contain *v.* съдържам [sudurzham]
contemplate *v.* размишлявам [razmish-lyavam], съзерцавам [suzertsavam]
continue *v.* продължавам [produlzhavam]
contract *n.* договор [dogovor]
converse *v.* говоря [govorya], разговарям [razgovaryam]; беседвам [besedvam]
cook *v.* готвя [gotvya]

cookie *n.* бисквита [biskvita], курабийка [kourabiyka]
cool *adj.* хладен [hladen]
copy *n.* копие [kopie]
corn *n.* царевица [tsarevitsa]
correct *adj.* правилен [pravilen]
corridor *n.* коридор [koridor]
cost *n.* цена [tsena]
costly *adj.* скъп [skup]
cotton *n.* памук [pamouk]
cough *n.* кашлица [kashlitsa]
country *n.* страна [strana]
cover *n.* капак [kapak]
cream *n.* сметана [smetana]
credit *n.* кредит [kredit]
creditor *n.* кредитор [kreditor]
cricket *n.* (*insect*) щурец [shturets]; (*sport*) крикет [kriket]
critical *adj.* критичен [kritichen]
croquet *n.* крокет [kroket]
cruel *adj.* жесток [zhestok]
cry *n.* вик [vik]; плач [plach]
crystal *n.* кристал [kristal]
cucumber *n.* краставица [krastavitsa]
cultural *adj.* културен [koultouren]
cup *n.* чаша [chasha]
cure *n.* лек [lek]; лечение [lechenie]; *v.* лекувам [lekuvam]
curry *n.* къри [kuri]
curtain *n.* перде [perde]
cut *n.* порязване [poryazvane]; парче [parche]; *v.* порязвам се [poryazvam se]
cute *adj.* хитър [hitur]; мил [mil], сладък [sladuk]; готин [gotin]
cutlet *n.* котлет [kotlet]
Czech *adj.* чешки [cheshki]

D

daily *adj.* ежедневен [ezhedneven]
dairy *n.* млекарница [mlekarnitsa]
dam *n.* язовир [yazovir]
damage *n.* повреда [povreda]
dance *n.* танц [tants]
dandruff *n.* пърхут [purhout]
danger *n.* опасност [opasnost]
dark *adj.* тъмен [tumen]
darling *n.* любимец [lyubimets]
date *n.* дата [data]; среща [sreshta]
day *n.* ден [den]
deadline *n.* краен срок [kraen srok]
deal *n.* споразумение [sporazoumenie], сделка [sdelka]
dear *adj.* драг [drag], мил [mil], скъп [skup]
debate *n.* дискусия [diskousiya], обсъждане [obsuzhdane]
debt *n.* дълг [dulg]
December *n.* декември [dekemvri]
decide *v.* решавам [reshavam]
decorate *v.* украсявам [oukrasyavam]
decrease *n.* понижавам [ponizhavam], намалявам [namalyavam]
deep *adj.* дълбок [dulbok]
deeply *adv.* дълбоко [dulboko]
defeat *n.* поражение [porazhenie]
defect *n.* недостатък [nedostatuk]
defend *v.* браня [branya]
definitely *adv.* определено [opredeleno], със сигурност [sus sigournost]
degree *n.* степен [stepen]
delay *n.* закъснение [zakusnenie]
demand *n.* искане [iskane]
dental *adj.* зъбен [zuben]

dentist *n.* зъболекар [zubolekar]
deny *v.* отричам [otricham]
depart *v.* тръгвам [trugvam], заминавам [zaminavam]
departure *n.* заминаване [zaminavane]
depend *v.* завися [zavisya]
deposit *n.* депозит [depozit]
depth *n.* дълбочина [dulbochina]
descend *v.* спускам се [spouskam se]
descent *n.* слизане [slizane]
design *n.* дизайн [dizayn]
designate *v.* обозначавам [oboznachavam], определям [opredelyam]
designer *n.* проектант [proektant]
desk *n.* писалище [pisalishte]; катедра [katedra]
dessert *n.* десерт [desert]
destroy *v.* унищожавам [ounishtozhavam]
detail *n.* детайл [detail]
determine *v.* определям [opredelyam]
develop *v.* развивам [razvivam]
devote *v.* посвещавам [posveshtavam]
dew *n.* роса [rosa]
diaper *n.* пелена [pelena]
diarrhea *n.* разстройство [razstroystvo], диария [diariya]
diary *n.* дневник [dnevnik]
dictionary *n.* речник [rechnik]
diet *n.* диета [dieta], храна [hrana]
difference *n.* разлика [razlika]
difficult *adj.* труден [trouden]
dig *v.* копая [kopaya]
digest *n.* сборник [sbornik]
dignify *v.* удостоявам [udostoyavam], въздигам [vuzdigam]
dignity *n.* достойнство [dostoynstvo]

dine *v.* обядвам [obyadvam], вечерям [vecheryam]
dinner *n.* обед [obed], вечеря [vecherya]
direct *v.* ръководя [rukovodya]; *adj.* директен [direkten], пряк [pryak]
director *n.* директор [direktor]
dirt *n.* мръсотия [mrusotiya]
dirty *adj.* мръсен [mrusen]
disagree *v.* не съвпадам [ne suvpadam]; не съм съгласен [ne sum suglasen]
disappear *v.* изчезвам [izchezvam]
disappoint *v.* разочаровам [razocharovam]
discount *n.* намаление [namalenie]
discover *v.* откривам [otkrivam]
dish *n.* чиния [chiniya]
diskette *n.* дискета [disketa]
dislike *n.* отвращение [otvrashtenie]
disperse *v.* разпилявам [razpilyavam]
display *n.* изложба [izlozhba]
dispute *n.* дискусия [diskousiya]; спор [spor]
dissolve *v.* разтварям [raztvaryam], разтопявам [raztopyavam]
distance *n.* разстояние [razstoyanie]
disturb *v.* безпокоя [bezpokoya]; смущавам [smoushtavam]
divide *v.* деля [delya]
divorce *n.* развод [razvod]
do *v.* правя [pravya]
doctor *n.* доктор [doktor], лекар [lekar]
dog *n.* куче [kouche]
doll *n.* кукла [koukla]
domestic *adj.* домашен [domashen]
donate *v.* дарявам [daryavam]
door *n.* врата [vrata]
dormitory *n.* общежитие [obshtezhitie]
double *adj.* двоен [dvoen]

down *adv.* долу [dolou]
downtown *n.* градски център [gradski tsentur]
draw *v.* рисувам [risouvam]
drawing *n.* рисунка [risounka]
dream *n.* сън [sun]
dress *n.* рокля [roklya]
drink *n.* напитка [napitka]; *v.* пия [piya]
drinking *n.* пиене [piene]
drive *n.* път [put]; *v.* карам [karam]
driver *n.* шофьор [shofyor]
drop *n.* капка [kapka]; *v.* капя [kapya]; изпускам [izpuskam]
drought *n.* суша [sousha]
drug *n.* лекарство [lekarstvo]
drugstore *n.* аптека [apteka]
drunk *adj.* пиян [piyan]
dry *adj.* сух [souh]
during *prep.* по време на [po vreme na]
dusk *n.* привечер [privecher]; здрач [zdrach]
dust *n.* прах [prah]
duty *n.* задължение [zadulzhenie]

E

each *adj.* всеки [vseki]
ear *n.* ухо [ouho]
earring *n.* обица [obitsa]
earth *n.* земя [zemya]
east *n.* изток [iztok]
Easter *n.* Великден [Velikden]
easy *adj.* лесен [lesen]
eat *v.* ям [yam]
edge *n.* ръб [rub]
edition *n.* издание [izdanie]
educate *v.* образовам [obrazovam]

education *n.* образование [obrazovanie]
egg *n.* яйце [yaytse]
eight *num.* осем [osem]
either *adj.* и единият, и другият [i ediniyat, i drugiyat], който и да е [koyto i da e]
elastic *adj.* еластичен [elastichen]
electricity *n.* електричество [elektrich-estvo]
electronics *n.* електроника [elektronika]
elegant *adj.* елегантен [eleganten]
elevator *n.* асансьор [asansyor]
else *adj.* друг [droug]
e-mail *n.* електронна поща [elektronna poshta]
embark *v.* тръгвам на път [trugvam na put]
emission *n.* емисия [emisiya]
employment *n.* работа [rabota]
empty *adj.* празен [prazen]
enclose *v.* ограждам [obgrazhdam]
encourage *v.* окуражавам [okourazhavam]
end *n.* край [kray]
energy *n.* енергия [energiya]
engage *v.* задължавам (се) [zadulzhavam (se)]; **get ~ed** сгодявам се [sgodyavam se]
engaged *adj.* сгоден [sgoden]
English *adj.* английски [angliyski]; *n.* (*language*) английски език [angliyski ezik]
enjoy *v.* радвам се [radvam se]
enough *adv.* стига [stiga]
entertainment *n.* забавление [zabavlenie]
entire *adj.* цял [tsyal]
entry *n.* влизане [vlizane]
envelope *n.* плик [plik]

equal *adj.* равен [raven], еднакъв [ednakuv], същ [susht]
era *n.* ера [era]
escape *n.* бягство [byagstvo]
esplanade *n.* променада [promenada]
evaluate *v.* оценявям [otsenyavam]
eve *n.* навечерие [navecherie]
even *adj.* равен [raven]
evening *n.* вечер [vecher]
event *n.* случка [slouchka]
every *adj.* всеки [vseki]
everyday *adj.* всеки ден [vseki den]
evidence *n.* доказателство [dokazatelstvo]
examination *n.* изследване [izsledvane]; изпит [izpit]
example *n.* пример [primer]
excellent *adj.* отличен [otlichen]
except *prep.* освен [osven]
exception *n.* изключение [izklyuchenie]
exceptional *adj.*изключителен [izklyuchitelen]
exchange *n.* смяна [smyana]; обмяна [obmayana]
exhibition *n.* изложба [izlozhba]
exit *n.* изход [izhod]
expect *v.* очаквам [ochakvam]
expensive *adj.* скъп [skup]
expert *n.* професионалист [profesionalist]
explain *v.* обяснявам [obyasnyavam]
extra *adj.* екстра [ekstra]
extraordinary *adj.* необикновен [neobiknoven]
eye *n.* око [oko]
eyedrops *n. pl.* капки за очи [kapki za ochi]

F

fable *n.* басня [basnya]
fabric *n.* тъкан [tukan], материал [material]
fabricate *v.* произвеждам [proizvezh-dam]; измислям [izmislyam]
face *n.* лице [litse]
facilitate *v.* улеснявам [ulesnyavam], правя възможно [pravya vuzmozhno]
fact *n.* факт [fakt]
factory *n.* фабрика [fabrika]
fad *n.* хит [hit], мода [moda]
faint *adj.* слаб [slab]
fail *v.* провалям се [provalyam se]
fair *adj.* справедлив [spravedliv]
faith *n.* вяра [vyara]; доверие [doverie]
fall *n.* есен [esen]; падане [padane]; *v.* падам [padam]
fame *n.* слава [slava]
family *n.* семейство [semeystvo]
famine *n.* глад [glad]
famous *adj.* известен [izvesten]
fan *n.* запалянко [zapalyanko]; ветрило [vetrilo], вентилатор [ventilator]
far *adv.* далеч [dalech], далеко [daleko]
faraway *adj.* далечен [dalechen]
farewell *n.* прощаване [proshtavane], сбогуване [sbogouvane]
farm *n.* ферма [ferma]
farmer *n.* фермер [fermer]
farther *adv.* по-нататък [po-natatuk]
fashion *n.* мода [moda]
fast *adj.* бърз [burz]
fat *adj.* мазен [mazen]; дебел [debel]
father *n.* баща [bashta]
fatigue *n.* умора [oumora]

feast *n.* угощение [ougoshtenie]
February *n.* февруари [fevrouari]
fee *n.* такса [taksa]
feed *n.* хранене [hranene]; храна [hrana]
feeling *n.* осезание [osezanie]; чувство [chuvstvo]
fellowship *n.* дружба [druzhba], приятелство [priyatelstvo]
female *adj.* женски [zhenski]; *n.* жена [zhena]; ~ **animal** самка [samka]
fence *n.* ограда [ograda]
festive *adj.* празничен [praznichen]
fetch *v.* донасям [donasyam]
fever *n.* треска [treska]
few *adv.* малко [malko]
fiction *n.* проза [proza]
field *n.* поле [pole]
fight *n.* борба [borba]; *v.* боря се [borya se]
figure *n.* фигура [figoura]
fill *v.* пълня [pulnya]
film *n.* филм [film]
final *adj.* краен [kraen]
finally *adv.* накрая [nakraya], окончателно [okonchatelno]
finance *n.* финанси [finansi]
find *v.* намирам [namiram]
fine *adj.* хубав [houbav]
finger *n.* пръст [prust]
finish *n.* край [kray]
fire *n.* огън [ogun]
firm *adj.* твърд [tvurd]; *n.* фирма [firma]
first *adj.* първи [purvi]
fish *n.* риба [riba]
fit *v.* пасвам [pasvam]
five *num.* пет [pet]
fix *v.* поправям [popravyam], оправям [opravyam]

flag *n.* знаме [zname]
flat *adj.* плосък [plosuk]; *n.* жилище [zhilishte]
flesh *n.* плът [plut]
flight *n.* полет [polet]
floor *n.* под [pod]
flour *n.* брашно [brashno]
flow *n.* поток [potok]; *v.* тека [teka]
flower *n.* цвете [tsvete]
fly *v.* летя [letya]
foam *n.* пяна [pyana]
focus *v.* фокусирам [fokousiram]
fog *n.* мъгла [mugla]
fold *n.* гънка [gunka]; *v.* сгъвам [sguvam]
folk *n. pl.* хора [hora], народ [narod]
follow *v.* следвам [sledvam]
following *adj.* следващ [sledvasht]
food *n.* храна [hrana]
foot *n.* крак [krak]
for *prep.* за [za]
forbid *v.* забранявам [zabranyavam]
force *n.* сила [sila]; *v.* насилвам [nasilvam], форсирам [forsiram]
forehead *n.* чело [chelo]
foreign *adj.* чужд [chouzhd]
forest *n.* гора [gora]
forever *adv.* завинаги [zavinagi]
forget *v.* забравям [zabravyam]
forgive *v.* прощавам [proshtavam]
form *n.* форма [forma]; *v.* формирам [formiram]
formal *adj.* формален [formalen]
formation *n.* формация [formatsiya]
former *adj.* бивш [bivsh]
forward *adv.* напред [napred]
foundation *n.* основа [osnova]
four *num.* четири [chetiri]

frame *n.* рамка [ramka]
free *adj.* свободен [svoboden]
freedom *n.* свобода [svoboda]
frequently *adv.* често [chesto]
fresh *adj.* пресен [presen]
Friday *n.* петък [petuk]
friend *n.* приятел [priyatel]
friendly *adj.* приятелски [priyatelski]
friendship *n.* приятелство [priyatelstvo]
from *prep.* от [ot]
front *n.* фронт [front]; *adj.* преден [preden]
fruit *n.* плод [plod]
fry *v.* пържа [purzha]
full *adj.* сит [sit]
fully *adv.* напълно [napulno], пълно [pulno]
function *n.* функция [founktsiya]
fund *n.* фонд [fond]
fundamental *adj.* основен [osnoven]
funny *adj.* смешен [smeshen]
further *adj.* следващ [sledvasht]
future *adj.* бъдещ [budesht]; *n.* бъдеще [budeshte]

G

gain *v.* печеля [pechelya]
game *n.* игра [igra]
gap *n.* дупка [doupka]; промеждутък [promezhdoutuk]
garage *n.* гараж [garazh]
garbage *n.* боклук [boklouk]
garden *n.* градина [gradina]
garlic *n.* чесън [chesun]
gas *n.* газ [gaz]
gasoline *n.* бензин [benzin]

gate *n.* врата [vrata]; вход [vhod]
gather *v.* събирам [subiram]
general *adj.* генерален [generalen]; *n.* генерал [general]
generally *adv.* обикновено [obiknoveno]; общо взето [obshto vzeto]
generate *v.* генерирам [generiram]
generation *n.* поколение [pokolenie], генерация [generatsiya]
gentleman *n.* джентълмен [dzhentulmen]
get *v.* получавам [polouchavam]
gift *n.* подарък [podaruk]
girl *n.* момиче [momiche]
give *v.* давам [davam]
glad *adj.* доволен [dovolen]
glance *v.* рикошира м [rikoshiram]; отразявам [otrazyavam], блестя [blestya]
glass *n.* стъкло [stuklo]
glove *n.* ръкавица [rukavitsa]
glue *n.* лепило [lepilo]
go *v.* отивам [otivam]
goal *n.* гол [gol] *(sports)*; цел [tsel]
gold *n.* злато [zlato]
good *adj.* добър [dobur]; *n.* добро [dobro]
Gothic *adj.* готически [goticheski]
goulash *n.* гулаш [goulash]
government *n.* правителство [pravitelstvo]
grammatical *adj.* граматически [gramaticheski]
grant *n.* стипендия [stipendiya]; *v.* давам [davam]
grape *n.* грозде [grozde]
grass *n.* трева [treva]
grateful *adj.* благодарен [blagodaren]

gravy *n.* сос [sos]
gray *adj.* сив [siv]
greasy *adj.* мазен [mazen]
great *adj.* голям [golyam]; велик [velik]
green *adj.* зелен [zelen]
greeting *n.* поздрав [pozdrav]
grill *v.* пека на скара [peka na skara]
grind *v.* меля [melya]
grocery *n.* бакалница [bakalnitsa]
ground *n.* земя [zemya]
group *n.* група [groupa]
grow *v.* раста [rasta]
growth *n.* растеж [rastezh]
guard *n.* стража [strazha]
guest *n.* гост [gost]
guide *n.* гид [gid]; ръководство [rukovodstvo]; *v.* водя [vodya]
guy *n.* момче [momche], човек [chovek]

H

hair *n.* коса [kosa]
half *n.* половина [polovina]
hall *n.* салон [salon]
ham *n.* шунка [shounka]
hand *n.* ръка [ruka]
handbag *n.* чанта [chanta]
handkerchief *n.* носна кърпа [nosna kurpa]
handle *v.* боравя с [boravya s], манипулирам [manipouliram]
hang *v.* закачвам [zakachvam]
happen *v.* случва се [slouchva se]
happy *adj.* щастлив [shtastliv]
hard *adv.* твърдо[tvurdo], кораво [koravo]; *adj.* корав [korav], твърд [tvurd]

hardly *adv.* едва [edva]
hat *n.* шапка [shapka]
hate *v.* мразя [mrazya]
have *v.* имам [imam]
hazelnut *n.* лешник [leshnik]
he *pron.* той [toy]
head *n.* глава [glava]; *v.* водя [vodya], възглавявам [vuzglavyavam]
heal *v.* лекувам [lekouvam]
health *n.* здраве [zdrave]
hear *v.* чувам [chouvam]
heart *n.* сърце [surtse]
heat *n.* топлина [toplina]
heavily *adv.* тежко [tezhko]
heavy *adj.* тежък [tezhuk]
height *n.* височина [visochina]
hello *interj.* здравей [zdravey]
help *n.* помощ [pomosht]; *v.* помагам [pomagam]
her *pron.* нея [neya], неин [nein]
here *adv.* тук [touk]
hide *v.* крия [kriya]
high *adj.* висок [visok]
highly *adv.* високо [visoko]
hill *n.* хълм [hulm]
his *pron.* негов [negov]
historic *adj.* исторически [istoricheski]
history *n.* история [istoriya]
hit *v.* удрям [oudryam]
hold *v.* държа [durzha]
hole *n.* дупка [doupka]
holiday *n.* празник [praznik]
home *n.* къща [kushta]
honey *n.* мед [med]
hope *n.* надежда [nadezhda]; *v.* надявам се [nadyavam se]
horse *n.* кон [kon]

hospital *n.* болница [bolnitsa]
hot *adj.* лютив [lyutiv]
hotel *n.* хотел [hotel]
hour *n.* час [chas]
house *n.* къща [kushta]; *v.* подслонявам [podslonyavam]
household *n.* домакинство [domakinstvo], покъщнина [pokushtnina]
how *adv.* как [kak]
however *adv.* както и да [kakto i da]; обаче [obache]
huge *adj.* огромен [ogromen]
human *adj.* човешки [choveshki]
hunger *n.* глад [glad]
hurry *n.* бързане [burzane]; *v.* бързам [burzam]
husband *n.* съпруг [suproug]

I

I *pron.* аз [az]
ice *n.* лед [led]
idea *n.* мисъл [misul], идея [ideya]
identify *v.* идентифицирам [identifitsiram]
identity *n.* самоличност [samolichnost]
if *conj.* ако [ako]
ill *adj.* болен [bolen]
illustrate *v.* илюстрирам [ilyustriram]
image *n.* образ [obraz]
imagine *v.* представям си [predstavyam si]
imitate *v.* имитирам [imitiram]
immediate *adj.* непосредствен [neposredstven], най-близък [nay-blizuk]
immediately *adv.* веднага [vednaga]
impact *n.* удар [oudar]; въздействие [vuzdeystvie]

imply *v.* съдържам [sudurzham], загатвам [zagatvam], подразбирам се [podrazbiram se]
importance *n.* важност [vazhnost]
important *adj.* важен [vazhen]
impose *v.* налагам [nalagam]
impossible *adj.* невъзможен [nevuzmozhen]
impression *n.* впечатление [vpechatlenie]
improve *v.* подобрявам се [podobryavam se]
improvement *n.* подобрение [podobrenie]
in *prep.* в [v]; *adv.* вътре [vutre]
incident *n.* случка [slouchka], произшествие [proizshestvie]
include *v.* включвам [vklyuchvam]
including *prep.* включително [vklyuchitelno]
income *n.* доход [dohod]
incorporate *v.* включвам [vklyuchvam]
increase *n.* растеж [rastezh]; *v.* увеличавам [ouvelichavam]
increasing *adj.* увеличаващ се [ouvelichavasht se]
indeed *adv.* в действителност [v deystvitel-nost], наистина [naistina]
independence *n.* независимост [nezavisimost]
independent *adj.* независим [nezavisim]
index *n.* индекс [indeks]
indicate *v.* посочвам [posochvam]
individual *n.* индивид [individ]
industrial *adj.* индустриален [indoustrialen]
industry *n.* индустрия [industriya]
inflation *n.* инфлация [inflatsiya]
influence *n.* влияние [vliyanie]; *v.* влияя [vliyaya]
inform *v.* информирам [informiram], осведомявам [osvedomyavam]

information *n.* информация [informat-siya]
initial *adj.* начален [nachalen]
initiative *n.* инициатива [initsiativa]
injury *n.* рана [rana]
ink *n.* мастило [mastilo]
inner *adj.* вътрешен [vutreshen]
inquiry *n.* разпитване [razpitvane]; следствие [sledstvie]
insect *n.* насекомо [nasekomo]
inside *adv.* вътрешно [vutreshno]
insist *v.* настоявам [nastoyavam]
instance *n.* пример [primer], отделен случай [otdelen sluchay]
instead *adv.* вместо [vmesto]
institute *n.* институт [institout]
institution *n.* институция [institoutsiya]
instruction *n.* инструкция [instroukt-siya]; обучение [obouchenie]
instrument *n.* инструмент [instroument]
insurance *n.* застраховка [zastrahovka]
intend *v.* възнамерявам [vuznameryavam]
intention *n.* намерение [namerenie]
interest *n.* интерес [interes]
interested *adj.* заинтересуван [zaintere-souvan]
interesting *adj.* интересен [interesen]
internal *adj.* вътрешен [vutreshen]
international *adj.* международен [mezhdounaroden]
interpret *v.* тълкувам [tulkouvam], обяснявам [obyasnyavam]
interpretation *n.* обяснение [obyasnenie]
interrupt *v.* прекъсвам [prekusvam]
interview *n.* интервю [intervyu]
into *prep.* в [v]
introduce *v.* въвеждам [vuvezhdam]

introduction *n.* увод [ouvod]
investigate *v.* изследвам [izsledvam]
investigation *n.* изследване [izsledvane]
investment *n.* инвестиция [investitsiya]
invite *v.* каня [kanya]
invoice *n.* фактура [faktoura]
involve *v.* включвам [vklyuchvam]
iron *v.* гладя [gladya]
island *n.* остров [ostrov]
issue *n.* издание [izdanie]; *v.* издавам [izdavam]
it *pron.* то [to]
item *n.* точка [tochka]

J

jacket *n.* сако [sako]
jam *n.* конфитюр [konfityur]
January *n.* януари [yanouari]
jealousy *n.* ревност [revnost]
job *n.* работа [rabota]
join *v.* съединявам [suedinyavam]
joint *n.* става [stava]
journey *n.* пътуване [putouvane]
joy *n.* радост [padost]
judge *n.* съдия [sudiya]; *v.* съдя [sudya]
July *n.* юли [yuli]
jump *v.* скачам [skacham]
June *n.* юни [yuni]
just *adv.* точно [tochno], тъкмо [tukmo]; справедлив [spravedliv]
justice *n.* справедливост [spravedlivost]

K

keep *v.* държа [durzha]
kettle *n.* метален чайник [metalen chaynik]
key *n.* ключ [klyuch]
kick *n.* ритник [ritnik]; *v.* ритам [ritam]
kid *n.* дете [dete]
kidney *n.* бъбрек [bubrek]
kill *v.* убивам [oubivam]
kind *n.* вид [vid]
king *n.* цар [tsar], крал [kral]
kiss *n.* целувка [tselouvka]
kitchen *n.* кухня [kouhnya]
knee *n.* коляно [kolyano]
kneel *v.* коленича [kolenicha]
knife *n.* нож [nozh]
knit *v.* плета [pleta]
knock *v.* удрям [oudryam], чукам [choukam]; *n.* чукване [choukvane]
know *v.* зная [znaya]
knowledge *n.* знание [znanie]

L

labor *n.* труд [troud]
lack *n.* липса [lipsa]
ladder *n.* стълба [stulba]
lady *n.* госпожа [gospozha]
lamb *n.* агне [agne]
lamp *n.* лампа [lampa]
land *n.* земя [zemya]; *v.* кацам [katsam]
language *n.* език [ezik]
large *adj.* голям [golyam]
last *adj.* последен [posleden]; *v.* продължавам [produlzhavam]
late *adj.* късен [kusen]

latter *adj.* по-късен [po-kusen]; втори [vtori]
laugh *v.* смея се [smeya se]
law *n.* закон [zakon]
lawyer *n.* адвокат [advokat]
lay *v.* поставям [postavyam]
lead *v.* водя [vodya]
leader *n.* ръководител [rukovoditel]
leaf *n.* лист [list], листо [listo]
learn *v.* уча се [oucha se]
least *adj.* най-малък [nai-maluk]
leave *v.* оставям [ostavyam]
left *adv.* ляво [lyavo]
leg *n.* крак [krak]
lemon *n.* лимон [limon]
length *n.* дължина [dulzhina]
less *adv.* по-малко [po-malko]
lesson *n.* урок [ourok]
let *v.* разрешавам [razreshavam]
letter *n.* писмо [pismo]
level *adj.* равен [raven]; *n.* ниво [nivo]
library *n.* библиотека [biblioteka]
lie *v.* лежа [lezha]
life *n.* живот [zhivot]
lift *n.* асансьор [asansyor]
light *n.* светлина [svetlina]; *v.* светвам [svetvam]
like *prep.* като [kato]; *v.* харесвам [haresvam]
limit *n.* граница [granitsa]
line *n.* линия [liniya]
link *n.* свръзка [svruzka], връзка [vruzka]
lion *n.* лъв [luv]
lip *n.* устна [oustna]
list *n.* списък [spisuk]; *v.* вписвам [vpisvam]
listen *v.* слушам [slousham]

little *adv.* малко [malko]
live *v.* живея [zhiveya]
liver *n.* черен дроб [cheren drob]
loan *n.* заем [zaem]
local *adj.* местен [mesten]
lock *n.* ключалка [klyuchalka]; *v.* заключвам [zaklyuchvam]
long *adj.* дълъг [dulug]
look *n.* поглед [pogled]; *v.* гледам [gledam]
lord *n.* господар [gospodar]
lose *v.* губя [goubya]
loss *n.* загуба [zagouba]
love *n.* любов [lyubov]; *v.* обичам [obicham]
lovely *adj.* разкошен [razkoshen]
low *adj.* нисък [nisuk]
lucky *adj.* щастлив [shtastliv]
lunch *n.* обед [obed]
lung *n.* бял дроб [byal drob]

M

machine *n.* машина [mashina]
madam *n.* госпожа [gospozha]
magazine *n.* списание [spisanie]
maid *n.* мома [moma]; прислужница [prislouzhnitsa]
mail *n.* поща [poshta]
main *adj.* главен [glaven]
make *v.* правя [pravya]
male *adj.* мъжки [muzhki]
man *n.* мъж [muzh], човек [chovek]
manage *v.* ръководя [rukovodya]
manager *n.* управител [oupravitel], началник [nachalnik]
many *adj.* много [mnogo]

map *n.* карта [karta]
March *n.* март [mart]
mark *n.* белег [beleg], знак [znak]; *v.* означавам [oznachavam]
market *n.* пазар [pazar]
marriage *n.* брак [brak], женитба [zhenitba], сватба [svatba]
marry *v.* женя [zhenya], оженвам [ozhenvam], омъжвам [omuzhvam]
match *n.* кибрит [kibrit]
matter *n.* материя [materiya]; материал [material]; значение [znachenie]
May *n.* май [may]
may *v.* мога [moga]
maybe *adv.* може би [mozhe bi]
me *pron.* мен [men]
meal *n.* ядене [yadene]
mean *v.* възнамерявам [vuznameryavam]; *adj.* среден [sreden]; подъл [podul]
meaning *n.* значение [znachenie]
meanwhile *adv.* междувременно [mezhdouvremenno]
measure *n.* мярка [myarka]
meat *n.* месо [meso]
mechanic *n.* механик [mehanik]
medical *adj.* медицински [meditsinski]
meet *v.* срещам [sreshtam]
meeting *n.* събиране [subirane]
member *n.* член [chlen]
membership *n.* членство [chlenstvo]
mention *v.* споменавам [spomenavam]
message *n.* съобщение [suobshtenie]
method *n.* метод [metod]
midday *n.* пладне [pladne]
middle *adj.* среден [sreden]
might *v.* бих могъл [bih mogul]
milk *n.* мляко [mlyako]

mind *n.* ум [oum], разум [razoum]; *v.* обръщам внимание на [obrushtam vnimanie na]
mine *n.* мина [mina]
minority *n.* малцинство [maltsinstvo]
minute *n.* минута [minouta]
mirror *n.* огледало [ogledalo]
Miss *n.* госпожица [gospozhitsa]
miss *v.* изпускам [izpouskam]
mistake *n.* грешка [greshka]
mix *v.* смесвам [smesvam]
modern *adj.* модерен [moderen]
Monday *n.* понеделник [ponedelnik]
money *n.* пари [pari]
month *n.* месец [mesets]
more *adv.* повече [poveche]
morning *n.* сутрин [soutrin]
most *adv.* най-много [nay-mnogo]
mother *n.* майка [mayka]
motor *n.* мотор [motor]
mountain *n.* планина [planina]
mouth *n.* уста [ousta]
move *v.* движа се [dvizha se]
movement *n.* движение [dvizhenie]
Mr. *n.* господин (г-н) [gospodin (g-n)]
Mrs. *n.* госпожа (г-жа) [gospozha (g-zha)]
much *adv.* много [mnogo]
museum *n.* музей [mouzey]
mushroom *n.* гъба [guba]
music *n.* музика [mouzika]
must *v.* трябва [tryabva]

N

nail *n.* нокът [nokut]
name *n.* име [ime]; *v.* назовавам [nazovavam]

narrow *adj.* тесен [tesen]
national *adj.* народен [naroden]
natural *adj.* природен [priroden]
nature *n.* природа [priroda]
near *prep.* наблизо [nablizo]
nearby *adj.* недалеко [nedaleko]
necessary *adj.* необходим [neobhodim]
neck *n.* врат [vrat]
need *n.* нужда [nouzhda]; *v.* нуждая се [nouzhdaya se]
needle *n.* игла [igla]
negative *adj.* негативен [negativen]
neighbor *n.* съсед [sused]
neither *pron.* нито единият, нито другият [nito ediniyat, nito drougiyat]
network *n.* мрежа [mrezha]
never *adv.* никога [nikoga]
nevertheless *adv.* въпреки това [vupreki tova]
new *adj.* нов [nov]
news *n.* новина [novina]
newspaper *n.* вестник [vestnik]
next *adj.* следващ [sledvasht]
nice *adj.* хубав [houbav]
night *n.* нощ [nosht]
nine *num.* девет [devet]
no *adj.* никакъв [nikakuv]; *part.* не [ne]
nobody *pron.* никой [nikoy]
noise *n.* шум [shoum]
none *pron.* никой [nikoy]
noon *n.* пладне [pladne]
normal *adj.* нормален [normalen]
north *n.* север [sever]
nose *n.* нос [nos]
not *part.* не [ne]
note *n.* бележка [belezhka]; *v.* забелязвам [zabelyazvam], отбелязвам [otbelyazvam]

nothing *pron.* нищо [nishto]
notice *n.* съобщение [suobshtenie]
noun *n. gram.* съществително [sushtestvitelno]
November *n.* ноември [noemvri]
now *adv.* сега [sega]
nuclear *adj.* ядрен [yadren]
number *n.* число [chislo]
numeral *n. gram.* числително [chislitelno]
nurse *n.* медицинска сестра [meditsinska sestra]
nut *n.* ядка [yadka]

O

obey *v.* подчинявам се [podchinyavam se], слушам [slousham]
object *n.* предмет [predmet]
obligation *n.* задължение [zadulzhenie]
observation *n.* наблюдениие [nablyudenie]
observe *v.* наблюдавам [nablyudavam]
obtain *v.* получавам [polouchavam]
obvious *adj.* явен [yaven]
occasion *n.* случай [slouchay]
October *n.* октомври [oktomvri]
off *adv.* от [ot]; *prep.* от [ot]
offer *v.* предлагам [predlagam]; *n.* предложение [predlozhenie]
office *n.* офис [ofis], канцелария [kantselariya]
official *adj.* служебен [slouzheben], официален [ofitsialen]; *n.* чиновник [chinovnik]
often *adv.* често [chesto]
oil *n.* олио [olio]; машинно масло [mashinno maslo]

okay *interj.* добре [dobre]
old *adj.* стар [star]
on *prep.* на [na], върху [vurhou]
once *adv.* веднъж [vednuzh], едно време [edno vreme]
one *num.* един [edin]
onion *n.* лук [louk]
only *adv.* само [samo]
onto *prep.* на [na], върху [vurhou]
open *adj.* отворен [otvoren]; *v.* отварям [otvaryam]
opening *n.* отвор [otvor]
opinion *n.* мнение [mnenie]
opportunity *n.* възможност [vuzmozhnost]
opposition *n.* опозиция [opozitsiya], съпротива [suprotiva]
option *n.* опция [optsiya]
or *conj.* или [ili]
orange *n.* портокал [portokal]; *adj.* оранжев [oranzhev]
order *n.* ред [red]; поръчка [poruchka]; *v.* нареждам [narezhdam]; поръчвам [poruchvam]
ordinary *adj.* обикновен [obiknoven]
organization *n.* организация [organizat-siya]
organize *v.* организирам [organiziram]
original *adj.* първоначален [purvonachalen], оригинален [originalen]
other *adj., pron.* друг [droug]
otherwise *adv.* иначе [inache]
out *adv.* вън [vun]
outcome *n.* резултат [rezoultat]
outside *adv.* навън [navun]
oven *n.* фурна [fourna]
over *prep.* над [nad]

overtime *n.* извънреден труд [izvunreden troud]
own *adj.* свой [svoy]; *v.* притежавам [pritezhavam]
owner *n.* собственик [sobstvenik]

P

pack *v.* опаковам [opakovam]
package *n.* пакет [paket]
packet *n.* пакет [paket]
page *n.* страница [stranitsa]
pain *n.* болка [bolka]
paint *v.* боядисвам [boyadisvam]; *n.* боя [boya]
painting *n.* картина [kartina], живопис [zhivopis]
pair *n.* чифт [chift]
pan *n.* тиган [tigan]
pancake *n.* палачинка [palachinka]
pants *n. pl.* панталони [pantaloni]
paper *n.* хартия [hartiya]
parent *n.* родител [roditel]
park *n.* парк [park]; *v.* паркирам [parkiram]
parking *n.* паркинг [parking]
parliament *n.* парламент [parlament]
part *n.* част [chast]
particle *n. gram.* частица [chastitsa]
particular *adj.* специфичен [spetsifichen]
partly *adv.* частично [chastichno]
partner *n.* партньор [partnyor]
party *n.* партия [partiya]; прием [priem]
pass *v.* минавам [minavam]
passage *n.* пасаж [pasazh]
passenger *n.* пътник [putnik]
passport *n.* паспорт [pasport]

past *adj.* минал [minal]; *n.* минало [minalo]
path *n.* пътека [puteka]
patient *n.* пациент [patsient]
pay *n.* заплата [zaplata]; *v.* плащам [plashtam]
payment *n.* плащане [plashtane]
peace *n.* мир [mir]
peach *n.* праскова [praskova]
peanut *n.* фъстък [fustuk]
pen *n.* писалка [pisalka]
pencil *n.* молив [moliv]
people *n. pl.* хора [hora]
perfect *adj.* съвършен [suvurshen]
perform *v.* изпълнявам [izpulnyavam], представям [predstavyam]
performance *n.* представление [predstavlenie]
perhaps *adv.* може би [mozhe bi]
period *n.* период [period]
permanent *adj.* постоянен [postoyanen]
permit *n.* разрешение [razreshenie]; *v.* разрешавам [razreshavam]
person *n.* човек [chovek]
personal *adj.* личен [lichen]
pharmacy *n.* аптека [apteka]
phone *n.* телефон [telefon]
photograph *n.* снимка [snimka], фотография [fotografiya]
physician *n.* лекар [lekar]
pick *v.* бера [bera], избирам [izbiram]
picture *n.* картина [kartina]
piece *n.* парче [parche]
pill *n.* таблетка [tabletka]
pillow *n.* възглавница [vuzglavnitsa]
pineapple *n.* ананас [ananas]
pink *adj.* розов [rozov]

place *n.* място [myasto]; *v.* поставям [postavyam]
plan *n.* план [plan]; *v.* организирам [organiziram], планирам [planiram]
plane *n.* самолет [samolet]
plant *n.* растение [rastenie]
plate *n.* чиния [chiniya]
play *n.* игра [igra]; *v.* играя [igraya]
please *interj.* моля [molya]
pleasure *n.* удоволствие [oudovolstvie]
plum *n.* слива [sliva]
plural *n. gram.* множествено число [mnozhestveno chislo]
p.m. *n.* след обед [sled obed]
pocket *n.* джоб [dzhob]
point *n.* точка [tochka]
police *n.* полиция [politsiya]
policeman *n.* полицай [politsay]
pork *n.* свинско месо [svinsko meso]
porridge *n.* овесена каша [ovesena kasha]
port *n.* пристанище [pristanishte]
position *n.* положение [polozhenie]
possibility *n.* възможност [vuzmozhnost]
post *n.* поща [poshta]
postcard *n.* картичка [kartichka]
potato *n.* картоф [kartof]
potential *adj.* възможен [vuzmozhen]
poultry *n.* домашни птици [domashni ptitsi]
powder *n.* прах [prah]
power *n.* сила [sila]
praise *n.* похвала [pohvala]
preach *v.* проповядвам [propovyadvam]
preface *n.* увод [ouvod]
prefer *v.* предпочитам [predpochitam]

preparation *n.* подготовка [podgotovka]
prepare *v.* подготвям [podgotvyam]
preposition *n. gram.* предлог [predlog]
prescription *n.* рецепта [retsepta]
presence *n.* присъствие [prisustvie]
present *adj.* присъстващ [prisustvasht]; *n.* подарък [podaruk]; *v.* представям [predstavyam]
press *n.* преса [presa]
pressure *n.* налягане [nalyagane]
pretty *adj.* хубав [houbav]
prevent *v.* преча [precha]
previously *adv.* предишно [predishno]
price *n.* цена [tsena]
primary *adj.* първичен [purvichen]
prime *adj.* главен [glaven]
principle *n.* директор [director]
prior *adj.* предишен [predishen]
priority *n.* приоритет [prioritet]
prison *n.* затвор [zatvor]
prize *n.* печалба [pechalba]
probably *adv.* навярно [navyarno]
proceed *v.* отивам [otivam], преминавам [preminavam], продължавам [produlzhavam]
process *n.* процес [protses]
product *n.* продукт [prodoukt]
profession *n.* професия [profesiya]
profit *n.* изгода [izgoda]
progress *n.* напредък [napreduk]
project *n.* проект [proekt]
promise *v.* обещавам [obeshtavam]
promote *v.* повишавам [povishavam]
pronoun *n. gram.* местоимение [mestoimenie]
proper *adj.* собствен [sobstven]
proposal *n.* предложение [predlozhenie]

protect *v.* пазя [pazya]
protection *n.* защита [zashtita]
proud *adj.* горд [gord]
prove *v.* доказвам [dokazvam]
provide *v.* грижа се [grizha se]
provision *n.*снабдяване [snabdyavane]; *pl.* провизии [provizii]
pub *n.* кръчма [kruchma]
public *adj.* публичен [poublichen]
publication *n.* публикация [publikatsiya], издание [izdanie]
publish *v.* издавам [izdavam]
pull *v.* дърпам [durpam]
pumpkin *n.* тиква [tikva]
pursue *v.* преследвам [presledvam]
push *v.* бутам [boutam]
put *v.* слагам [slagam]

Q

quality *n.* качество [kachestvo]
quantity *n.* количество [kolichestvo]
quarrel *n.* кавга [kavga]
quarter *n.* четвъртина [chetvurtina]
queen *n.* царица [tsaritsa]
question *n.* въпрос [vupros]; *v.* питам [pitam], оспорвам [osporvam]
quick *adj.* бърз [burz]
quickly *adv.* бързо [burzo]
quiet *adj.* тих [tih]
quite *adv.* съвсем [suvsem]
quote *v.* цитирам [tsitiram]

R

rabbit *n.* заек [zaek]
race *n.* състезание [sustezanie]

railroad *n.* железница [zheleznitsa]
rain *n.* дъжд [duzhd]
raise *v.* вдигам [vdigam]
raisin *n.* стафида [stafida]
range *n.* обсег [obseg]
rapidly *adv.* бързо [burzo]
rare *adj.* рядък [ryaduk]
rather *adv.* по-скоро [po-skoro]
raw *adj.* суров [sourov]
reach *v.* достигам [dostigam]
read *v.* чета [cheta]
ready *adj.* готов [gotov]
real *adj.* истински [istinski]
realize *v.* осъзнавам [osuznavam]
reason *n.* довод [dovod]
reasonable *adj.* разумен [razoumen]
receipt *n.* разписка [razpiska]
receive *v.* получавам [polouchavam]
recently *adv.* неотдавна [neotdavna]
recognize *v.* разпознавам [razpoznavam]
recommend *v.* препоръчвам [preporuchvam]
record *n.* запис [zapis]
recover *v.* възстановявам [vuzstanovyavam]
red *adj.* червен [cherven]
reduce *v.* намалявам [namalyavam]
reference *n.* справка [spravka], сведение [svedenie]
refreshment *n.* освежаване [osvezhavane]
refrigerator *n.* хладилник [hladilnik]
refuse *v.* отказвам [otkazvam]
regard *v.* считам [schitam]
region *n.* област [oblast]
register *v.* записвам [zapisvam], вписвам [vpisvam]
regular *adj.* редовен [redoven]

reject *v.* отхвърлям [othvurlyam]
relationship *n.* връзка [vruzka]
religion *n.* религия [religiya]
remember *v.* спомням си [spomnyam si]
rent *n.* наем [naem]
repair *n.* поправка [popravka]
repeat *v.* повтарям [povtaryam]
reply *v.* отговарям [otgovaryam]
report *n.* доклад [doklad]
republic *n.* република [repoublika]
require *v.* изисквам [iziskvam]
research *n.* изследване [izsledvane]
resident *n.* жител [zhitel]
respect *n.* уважение [ouvazhenie]
respond *v.* отговарям [otgovaryam]
response *n.* отговор [otgovor]
rest *n.* почивка [pochivka]
restaurant *n.* ресторант [restorant]
return *n.* връщане [vrushtane]
rice *n.* ориз [oriz]
revolution *n.* революция [revolyutsiya]
right *adv.* направо [napravo]
ring *n.* пръстен [prusten]
river *n.* река [reka]
road *n.* път [put]
roof *n.* покрив [pokriv]; стряха [stryaha]
room *n.* стая [staya]
root *n.* корен [koren]
route *n.* маршрут [marshrut], път [put]
royal *adj.* царски [tsarski]
rule *n.* правило [pravilo]
run *n.* бягане [byagane], тичане [tichane]; *v.* тичам [ticham]
rural *adj.* селски [selski]

S

sack *n.* торба [torba]
safe *adj.* безопасен [bezopasen], сигурен [sigouren]
sale *n.* разпродажба [razprodazhba], продажба [prodazhba]
salt *n.* сол [sol]
same *adj.* същ [susht]
Saturday *n.* събота [subota]
sauce *n.* сос [sos]
save *v.* спасявам [spasyavam]
say *v.* казвам [kazvam]
scale *n.* скала [skala]
scene *n.* сцена [stsena]
school *n.* училище [ouchilishte]
science *n.* наука [naouka]
scissors *n.* ножица [nozhitsa]
sea *n.* море [more]
search *v.* търся [tursya]
season *n.* сезон [sezon], годишно време [godishno vreme]
seat *n.* стол [stol], място (за сядане) [myasto (za syadane)]
second *adj.* втори [vtori]
secretary *n.* секретарка [sekretarka]
security *n.* безопастност [bezopasnost]
see *v.* виждам [vizhdam]
seek *v.* търся [tursya]
seem *v.* изглеждам [izglezhdam]
sell *v.* продавам [prodavam]
send *v.* изпращам [izprashtam]
separate *adj.* отделен [otdelen]
September *n.* септември [septemvri]
series *n. pl.* редица [reditsa]
serious *adj.* сериозен [seriozen]
servant *n.* слуга [slouga]

service *n.* служба [slouzhba]
settle *v.* настанявам се [nastanyavam se]
seven *num.* седем [sedem]
several *adj.* няколко [nyakolko]
shadow *n.* сянка [syanka]
share *n.* акция (борсова) [aktsiya (borsova)]
she *pron.* тя [tya]
shift *v.* премествам [premestvam]
ship *n.* кораб [korab]
shoe *n.* обувка [obouvka]
shop *n.* магазин [magazin]
shopping *n.* пазаруване [pazarouvane]
short *adj.* кратък [kratuk]
shoulder *n.* рамо [ramo]
shout *v.* викам [vikam]
show *v.* показвам [pokazvam]
shut *v.* затварям [zatvaryam]
sick *n.* болен [bolen]
side *n.* страна [strana]
similarly *adv.* подобно [podobno]
simple *adj.* елементарен [elementaren], прост [prost]
sing *v.* пея [peya]
singer *n.* певец [pevets]
single *adj.* единичен [edinichen]
sink *n.* мивка [mivka]
sir *n.* господин [gospodin]
sister *n.* сестра [sestra]
sit *v.* седя [sedya]
six *num.* шест [shest]
size *n.* размер [razmer]
skill *n.* умение [oumenie]
skin *n.* кожа [kozha]
sky *n.* небе [nebe]
sleep *v.* спя [spya]
slow *adj.* бавен [baven]

small *adj.* малък [maluk]
smell *v.* мириша [mirisha]
smile *n.* усмивка [ousmivka]
smoke *v.* пуша [pousha]
so *adv.* така [taka]
soap *n.* сапун [sapoun]
soccer *n.* футбол [foutbol]
social *adj.* обществен [obshtestven]
soft *adj.* мек [mek]
soil *n.* почва [pochva]
soldier *n.* войник [voynik]
solution *n.* решение [reshenie]
some *adj.* някакъв [nyakakuv]
somewhere *adv.* някъде [nyakude]
son *n.* син [sin]
song *n.* песен [pesen]
soon *adv.* скоро [skoro]
sorry *interj.* извинете [izvinete], пардон [pardon]
sort *n.* вид [vid]
soup *n.* супа [soupa]
south *n.* юг [yug]
space *n.* място [myasto]
speak *v.* говоря [govorya]
specific *adj.* специфичен [spetsifichen]
speech *n.* реч [rech]
spend *v.* харча [harcha]
spice *n.* подправка [podpravka]
spinach *n.* спанак [spanak]
spoon *n.* лъжица [luzhitsa]
spot *n.* леке [leke], петно [petno]
spring *n.* пролет [prolet]
square *n.* площад [ploshtad]
stand *v.* стоя [stoya]
standard *n.* стандарт [standart]
star *n.* звезда [zvezda]
start *v.* започвам [zapochvam]

state *n.* състояние [sustoyanie]
statement *n.* твърдение [tvurdenie], изложение [izlozhenie]
station *n.* станция [stantsiya]
stay *v.* оставам [ostavam]
step *n.* крачка [krachka]
stick *v.* забождам [zabozhdam], намушвам [namoushvam]
still *adv.* все още [vse oshte]
stop *n.* спирка [spirka]; *v.* спирам [spiram]
store *n.* магазин [magazin]
story *n.* разказ [razkaz], история [istoriya]
street *n.* улица [oulitsa]
streetcar *n.* трамвай [tramvay]
strong *adj.* силен [silen]
study *v.* уча [oucha]
subject *n. gram.* подлог [podlog]
subway *n.* метро [metro]
succeed *v.* успявам [ouspyavam]
success *n.* успех [ouspeh]
successful *adj.* успешен [ouspeshen]
such *adj.* такъв [takuv]
sugar *n.* захар [zahar]
suit *n.* костюм [kostyum]
suitable *adj.* подходящ [podhodyasht]
suitcase *n.* куфар [koufar]
summer *n.* лято [lyato]
sun *n.* слънце [sluntse]
Sunday *n.* неделя [nedelya]
sunrise *n.* изгрев [izgrev]
sunset *n.* залез [zalez]
supermarket *n.* супермаркет [souper-market]
supper *n.* вечеря [vecherya]
suppose *v.* предполагам [predpolagam]

sure *adj.* сигурен [sigouren]
surname *n.* презиме [prezime]
surprise *n.* изненада [iznenada]
sweater *n.* пуловер [poulover]
sweet *adj.* сладък [sladuk]
swim *v.* плувам [plouvam]
swimming pool *n.* басейн [baseyn]
switch *n.* превключвател [prevklyuchvatel]
syrup *n.* сироп [sirop]

T

table *n.* маса [masa]
take *v.* вземам [vzemam]
talk *n.* разговор [razgovor]; *v.* говоря [govorya]
tall *adj.* висок [visok]
tape *n.* лента [lenta]
taste *n.* вкус [vkous]; *v.* вкусвам [vkousvam]
tax *n.* данък [danuk]
taxi *n.* такси [taksi]
tea *n.* чай [chay]
teach *v.* обучавам [obouchavam]
teacher *n.* учител [ouchitel]
tear *v.* късам [kusam]; **(from eye)** *n.* сълза [sulza]
telephone *n.* телефон [telefon]
tell *v.* казвам [kazvam]
temperature *n.* температура [temperatoura]
ten *num.* десет [deset]
term *n.* период [period]
texture *n.* тъкан [tukan]
thank *v.* благодаря [blagodarya]
thanks *n.* благодарности [blagodarnosti]

theater *n.* театър [teatur]
them *pron.* тях [tyah], ги [gi]
then *adv.* тогава [togava]
there *adv.* там [tam]
they *pron.* те [te]
thick *adj.* дебел [debel]
thin *adj.* тънък [tunuk]
thing *n.* нещо [neshto]
think *v.* мисля [mislya]
thirst *n.* жажда [zhazhda]
thought *n.* мисъл [misul]
thread *n.* конец [konets]
three *num.* три [tri]
throat *n.* гърло [gurlo]
through *prep.* през [prez]
throughout *prep.* навсякъде [navsyakude]
throw *v.* хвърлям [hvurlyam]
Thursday *n.* четвъртък [chetvurtuk]
ticket *n.* билет [bilet]
ticket office *n.* каса [kasa]
time *n.* време [vreme]
tip *n.* бакшиш [bakshish]
tire *n.* гума [gouma]
tired *adj.* изморен [izmoren]
toast *n.* препечена филийка [prepechena filiyka]
tobacco *n.* тютюн [tyutyun]
today *adv.* днес [dnes]
toe *n.* пръст на крак [prust na krak]
together *adv.* заедно [zaedno]
toilet *n.* тоалетна [toaletna]
toilet paper *n.* тоалетна хартия [toaletna hartiya]
tomato *n.* домат [domat]
tomorrow *adv.* утре [outre]
tongue *n.* език [ezik]
tooth *n.* зъб [zub]

toothbrush *n.* четка за зъби [chetka za zubi]
toothpaste *n.* паста за зъби [pasta za zubi]
total *adj.* цялостен [tsyalosten]
touch *n.* допир [dopir]; *v.* докосвам [dokosvam]
tour *n.* тур [tour]
towards *prep.* към [kum]
towel *n.* кърпа[kurpa]
tower *n.* кула [koula]
town *n.* град [grad]
toy *n.* играчка [igrachka]
trade *n.* търговия [turgoviya]
tradition *n.* традиция [traditsiya]
traffic *n.* трафик [trafik]
train *n.* влак [vlak]
tram *n.* трамвай [tramvay]
transport *n.* транспорт [transport]
travel *n.* пътуване [putouvane]; *v.* пътувам [putouvam]
treat *v.* лекувам [lekouvam]
treatment *n.* лечение [lechenie]
tree *n.* дърво [durvo]
trend *n.* мода [moda]
trip *n.* пътуване [putouvane]
trouble *n.* беда [beda]
trousers *n.* панталон [pantalon]
true *adj.* правдив [pravdiv]
trust *n.* доверие [doverie]; *v.* доверявам се [doveryavam se]
truth *n.* истина [istina]
try *v.* опитвам [opitvam]
Tuesday *n.* вторник [vtornik]
turn *n.* обръщане [obrushtane]; *v.* обръщам [obrushtam], въртя (се) [vurtya (se)]

twice *adv.* два пъти [dva puti]
two *num.* две [dve]

U

ugly *adj.* грозен [grozen]
umbrella *n.* чадър [chadur]
unable *adj.* неспособен [nesposoben]
under *prep.* под [pod]
understand *v.* разбирам [razbiram]
unemployment *n.* безработица [bezrabotitsa]
unfortunately *adv.* за жалост [za zhalost]
union *n.* съюз [suyuz]
unite *v.* съединявам [suedinyavam]
university *n.* университет [ouniversitet]
unknown *adj.* непознат [nepoznat]
unlock *v.* отключвам [otklyuchvam]
until *prep.* докато [dokato]
unusual *adj.* необикновен [neobiknoven]
up *adv.* нагоре [nagore]
upper *adj.* горен [goren]
urban *adj.* градски [gradski]
urgent *adj.* неотложен [neotlozhen]
urine *n.* урина [ourina]
use *v.* употребявам [oupotrebyavam]
useful *adj.* полезен [polezen]
usual *adj.* обикновен [obiknoven]

V

vacation *n.* ваканция [vakantsiya]
vaccination *n.* ваксинация [vaksinatsiya]
value *n.* стойност [stoynost], ценност [tsennost]
variation *n.* вариация [variatsiya]
variety *n.* разнообразие [raznoobrazie],

множество [mnozhestvo]; вариете [variete]
vase *n.* ваза [vaza]
vast *adj.* огромен [ogromen], обширен [obshiren]
veal *n.* телешко месо [teleshko meso]
vegetable *n.* зеленчук [zelenchouk]
vehicle *n.* превозно средство [prevozno sredstvo]
vein *n.* вена [vena]
venison *n.* еленско месо [elensko meso]
verb *n. gram.* глагол [glagol]
vertebra *n.* прешлен [preshlen]
vertigo *n.* световъртеж [svetovurtezh]
very *adv.* много [mnogo]
via *prep.* през [prez]
victory *n.* победа [pobeda]
view *n.* гледка [gledka]; *v.* гледам [gledam]
village *n.* село [selo]
vinegar *n.* оцет [otset]
vision *n.* зрение [zrenie]
visit *n.* посещение [poseshtenie]; *v.* посещавам [poseshtavam]
vital *adj.* жизнен [zhiznen]
voice *n.* глас [glas]
vomit *v.* повръщам [povrushtam]
vote *n.* гласуване [glasouvane]; *v.* гласувам [glasouvam]

W

wage *n.* заплата [zaplata]
waist *n.* кръст [krust]
wait *v.* чакам [chakam]
waiter *n.* сервитьор [servityor]
wake up *v.* събуждам се [subouzhdam se]

walk *v.* ходя [hodya]
wall *n.* стена [stena]
wallet *n.* портмоне [portmone]
walnut *n.* орех [oreh]
want *v.* искам [iskam]
war *n.* война [voyna]
warm *adj.* топъл [topul]
warn *v.* предупреждавам [predouprezh-davam]
wary *adj.* предпазлив [predpazliv]
wash *v.* пера [pera]
washbowl *n.* мивка [mivka]
washing machine *n.* пералня [peralnya]
wasp *n.* оса [osa]
watch *v.* наблюдавам [nablyudavam]; *n.* часовник [chasovnik]
water *n.* вода [voda]
wave (on the water) *n.* вълна (във водата) [vulna (vuv vodata)]
way *n.* начин [nachin], път [put]
we *pron.* ние [nie]
weak *adj.* слаб [slab]
wear *v.* нося [nosya]
weather *n.* време [vreme]
Wednesday *n.* сряда [sryada]
week *n.* седмица [sedmitsa]
weekend *n.* края на седмицата [kraya na sedmitsata]
weigh *v.* претеглям [preteglyam]
weight *n.* тегло [teglo]
welcome *v.* приветствам [privetstvam]
well *adv.* добре [dobre]
west *n.* запад [zapad]
wet *adj.* мокър [mokur]
what *pron.* какво [kakvo], що [shto]; какъв [kakuv]
when *adv.* кога [koga]

where *adv.* къде [kude], где [gde], откъде [otkude]
which *pron.* кой [koy], който [koyto]
while *n.* момент [moment]
white *adj.* бял [byal]
who *pron.* кой [koy]
whole *adj.* цял [tsyal]
why *adv.* защо [zashto]
wide *adj.* широк [shirok]
wife *n.* съпруга [suprouga]
win *v.* печеля [pechelya]
wind *n.* вятър [vyatur]
window *n.* прозорец [prozorets]
wine *n.* вино [vino]
winter *n.* зима [zima]
wish *v.* желая [zhelaya]
with *prep.* с (със) [s (sus)]
without *prep.* без [bez]
woman *n.* жена [zhena]
wonderful *adj.* прекрасен [prekrasen]
wood *n.* гора [gora]
wool *n.* вълна [vulna]
word *n.* дума [duma]
work *n.* работа [rabota]; *v.* работя [rabotya]
worker *n.* работник [rabotnik]
world *n.* свят [svyat]
wound *n.* рана [rana]
wrap *v.* завивам [zavivam]
wrapper *n.* опаковка [opakovka]
write *v.* пиша [pisha]
writer *n.* писател [pisatel]
writing *n.* писане [pisane]
wrong *adj.* грешен [greshen]

X

X-ray *n.* рентгенов лъч [rengenov luch]

Y

yard *n.* двор [dvor]
year *n.* година [godina]
yellow *adj.* жълт [zhult]
yes *adv.* да [da]
yesterday *adv.* вчера [vchera]
yet *adv.* още [oshte]; вече [veche]
yolk *n.* жълтък [zhultuk]
you *pron.* ти [ti], вие [vie]
young *adj.* млад [mlad]
your *adj.* твой [tvoy]; ваш [vash]
yours *pron.* твой [tvoy], ваш [vash]
youth *n.* младост [mladost]

Z

zero *n.* нула [noula]
zodiac *n.* зодиак [zodiak]
zoo *n.* зоологическа градина [zoologicheska gradina]

PHRASEBOOK

NOTE

Throughout the phrasebook we use the following formats:

When the subject can be omitted in the Bulgarian, it is shown in parentheses. The shorter form, without the subject, is often used in conversations. If the word order changes in the shorter form, both are given:

I speak a little Bulgarian.
(Аз) зная малко български.
[(Az) znaya malko bulgarski.]

I am tired.
Аз съм изморен|а. [Az sum izmoren|a.]
Изморен|а съм. [Izmoren|a sum.]

In order to differentiate singular and plural verb forms, the verb up to a | is the singular form, the letter(s) after the | is/are added to form the plural. For example:

Listen.
Слушай|те. [Sloushay|te.]

The singular verb is: **Слушай**, and the plural verb is: **Слушайте**.

When the addition of a suffix is used to differentiate masculine from feminine, the word is given with a | before the feminine suffix. For example:

I want …
(Аз) бих искал|а … [(Az) bih iskal|a …]

If a vowel should be omitted when forming the feminine that vowel is underlined. For example:

I am hungry.
Гладен|а съм. [Gladen|a sum.]
(гладен|а → full form: гладен *m.* / гладна *f.* [gladen/gladna])

I am thirsty.
Жаден|а съм. [Zhaden|a sum.]
(жаден|а → full form: жаден *m.* / жадна *f.* [zhaden / zhadna])

If you have a choice between two words in a sentence, the two words are divided by one slashes. For example:

And you? **А вие/ти?**
("And you?" can be translated "А вие?" or "А ти?")

ETIQUETTE & BASICS

Greetings and Goodbyes

Good morning.
Добро утро. [Dobro outro.]

Good afternoon.
Добър ден. [Dobur den.]

Good evening.
Добър вечер. [Dobur vecher.]

Hi. / Hello.
Здравей. [Zdravey.]
Здравейте. [Zdraveyte.]

Goodbye.
Довиждане. [Dovizhdane.]

See you soon.
До скоро. [Do skoro.]

Bye.
Чао. [Chao.]

Good night.
Лека нощ. [Leka nosht.]

Polite Expressions

How are you?
sing. **Как си?** [Kak si?]
Как се чустваш?
[Kak se choustvash?]

pl. **Как сте?** [Kak ste?]
Как се чувствате?
[Kak se chouvstvate?]

I am fine, thanks. And you?
Благодаря, добре. А Вие/ти?
[Blagodarya, dobre. A Vie/ti?]
Аз съм добре, благодаря. А Вие/ти?
[Az sum dobpe, blagodarya. A Vie/ti?]

Please.
Моля. [Molya.]

Many thanks.
Много благодаря.
[Mnogo blagodarya.]
Много Ви/ти благодаря.
[Mnogo Vi/ti blagodarya.]

You are welcome.
За нищо. [Za nishto.]

Excuse me!
Извинете! [Izvinete!]

Sorry.
Извинявам се. [Izvinyavam se.]
Аз се извинявам. [Az se izvinyavam.]

I apologize in advance.
Извинявам Ви/ти се предварително.
[Izvinyavam Vi/ti se predvaritelno.]
Предварително Ви/ти се извинявам.
[Predvaritelno Vi/ti se izvinyavam.]

It does not matter.
Няма значение. [Nyama znachenie.]

All right.
Добре. [Dobre.]

Special Occasion Expressions

Congratulations!
Честито! [Chestito!]

Happy birthday!
Честит Рожден Ден!
[Chestit Pozhden Den!]

Merry Christmas and Happy New Year.
Весела Коледа и щастлива Нова Година.
[Vesela Koleda i shtastliva Nova Godina.]

Happy Easter.
Честит Великден. [Chestit Velikden.]

I wish you a lot of success.
Пожелавам Ви/ти много успехи.
[Pozhelavam Vi/ti mnogo ouspehi.]
Аз Ви/ти пожелавам много успехи.
[Az Vi/ti pozhelavam mnogoouspehi]

Useful Expressions

Is that so?
Така ли е? [Taka li e?]

I would like …
(Аз) бих искал|а … [(Az) bih iskal|a …]

I do not want …
(Аз) не искам … [(Az) ne iskam …]

Where is …
Къде е … [Kude e …]

When does it …?
Кога …? [Koga …?]
open **отваря** [otvarya]
close **затваря** [zatvarya]

I am looking for …
(Аз) търся … [(Az) tursya …]

Can you recommend a …
Можете ли да ми препоръчате …
[Mozhete li da mi preporuchate …]
Можете ли да ме посъветвате …
[Mozhete li da me posuvetvate …]

Can you help me, please?
Можете ли да ми помогнете, моля?
[Mozhete li da mi pomognete, molya?]

Good.
Добре. [Dobre.]

It is bad.
Това е лошо. [Tova e losho.]

It's my fault.
Това е моя грешка. [Tova e moya greshka.]

It's not my fault.
Това не е моя грешка.
[Tova ne e moya greshka.]

I know.
(Аз) знам. [(Az) znam.]

I don't know.
(Аз) не знам. [(Az) ne znam.]

Wait a minute.
Изчакайте малко. [Izchakayte malko.]
Почакайте малко. [Pochakayte malko.]

A minute, please.
Минута, моля. [Minouta, molya.]

Come in. **Влезте.** [Vlezte.]
Come here. **Елате тук.** [Elate touk.]
Go there. **Отидете там.** [Otidete tam.]
Stop here. **Спрете тук.** [Sprete touk.]

Welcome. **Добре дошли.** [Dobre doshli.]

Can I help you?
Мога ли да Ви помогна?
[Moga li da Vi pomogna?]

What time is it?
Колко е часът? [Kolko e chasut?]

What is wrong?
Какво не е наред? [Kakvo ne e nared?]

Listen.
Слушай|те. [Sloushay|te.]

Be careful!
Внимавай|те! [Vnimavay|te!]

Come quickly.
Ела|те бързо. [Ela|te burzo.]

I am hungry.
Гладен|а съм. [Gladen|a sum.]

I am thirsty.
Жаден|а съм. [Zhaden|a sum.]

I am not hungry.
Не съм гладен|а. [Ne sum gladen|a.]

I am not thirsty.
Не съм жаден|а. [Ne sum zhaden|a.]

I am full.
Нахраних се. [Nahranih se.]
Стига ми. [Stiga mi.]

I am sorry.
Извинете. [Izvinete.]

I am tired.
Аз съм изморен|а. [Az sum izmoren|a.]
Изморен|а съм. [Izmoren|a sum.]

I am sad.
Мъчно ми е. [Muchno mi e.]

I have got a cold.
Аз съм настинал|а. [Az sum nastinal|a.]
Настинал|а съм. [Nastinal|a sum.]

I am hot.
Горещо ми е. [Goreshto mi e.]

Questions

Who?	**Кой?** [Koy?]
Why?	**Защо?** [Zashto?]
When?	**Кога?** [Koga?]
Where?	**Къде?** [Kude?]
What?	**Какво?** [Kakvo?]
How?	**Как?** [Kak?]
Here.	**Тук.** [Touk.]
There.	**Там.** [Tam.]

What is that?
Какво е онова? [Kakvo e onova?]

What is this?
Какво е това? [Kakvo e tova?]

Who is that?
Кой е това? [Koy e tova?]

LANGUAGE

Do you speak English?
Говорите ли английски?
[Govodite li angliyski?]

Yes, I do.
Да, говоря. [Da, govorya.]

Just a bit.
Малко. [Malko.]

I don't speak English.
(Аз) не говоря английски.
[(Az) ne govorya angliyski.]

I don't speak Bulgarian.
(Аз) не зная български.
[(Az) ne znaya bulgarski.]
(Аз) не говоря български.
[(Az) ne govorya bulgarski.]

I do not know Bulgarian.
(Аз) не знам български.
[(Az) ne znam bulgarski.]

I speak a little Bulgarian.
(Аз) говоря малко български.
[(Az) govorya malko bulgarski.]

I don't understand.
(Аз) не разбирам. [(Az) ne razbiram.]

Could you speak more slowly, please?
Бихте ли говорил|а по-бавно, моля?
[Bihte li govoril|a po-bavno, molya?]

Could you repeat it, please?
Бихте ли го повторил|а, моля?
[Bihte li go povtoril|a, molya?]

Could you write that down, please?
Бихте ли го написал|а, моля?
[Bihte li go napisal|a, molya?]

What does that mean?
Какво означава?
[Kakvo oznachava?]

How do you say … in English?
Как ще се каже … на английски?
[Kak shte se kazhe … na angliyski?]

How do you say … in Bulgarian?
Как ще се каже … на български?
[Kak shte se kazhe … na bulgarski?]

How do you spell it?
Как се чете буква по буква?
[Kak se chete boukva po boukva?]

How do you pronounce this?
Как се произнася това?
[Kak se proiznasya tova?]

I know …
(Аз) знам … [(Az) znam …]

I speak
(Аз) говоря … [(Az) govorya …]

Bulgarian	**български** [bulgarski]
Czech	**чешки** [cheshki]
Dutch	**холандски** [holandski]

English	**английски** [angliyski]
French	**френски** [frenski]
German	**немски** [nemski]
Italian	**италиански** [italianski]
Polish	**полски** [poski]
Portuguese	**португалски** [portougalski]
Russian	**руски** [rouski]
Slovak	**словашки** [slovashki]
Spanish	**испански** [ispanski]

INTRODUCTIONS

Let me introduce myself.
Позволете ми да се представя.
[Pozvolete mi da se predstavya.]

My name is …
Казвам се … [Kazvam se …]

Nice to meet you.
Радвам се да се запознаем.
[Radvam se da se zapoznaem.]
Приятно ми е.
[Priyatno mi e.]

Do you know Mr./Mrs./Miss …
Познавате ли господин/госпожа/ госпожица …
[Poznavate li gospodin/gospozha/ gospozhitsa …]

What is your name?
Как се казвате?
[Kak se kazvate?]
Какво е Вашето/твоето име?
[Kakvo e Vaseto/tvoeto ime?]

I am from …
(Аз) съм от … [(Az) sum ot …]

America	**Америка** [Amerika]
Australia	**Австралия** [Avstraliya]
Canada	**Канада** [Kanada]
England	**Англия** [Angliya]

Other Countries

Albania	**Албания** [Albaniya]
Austria	**Австрия** [Avstriya]
Bulgaria	**България** [Bulgariya
Croatia	**Хърватско** [Hurvatsko]
Czech Republic	**Чехия** [Chehiya]
France	**Франция** [Frantsiya]
Germany	**Германия** [Germaniya]
Great Britain	**Великобритания** [Velikobritaniya]
Greece	**Гърция** [Gurtsiya]
Holland	**Холандия** [Holandiya]
Hungary	**Унгария** [Oungariya]
Ireland	**Ирландия** [Irlandiya]
Italy	**Италия** [Italiya]
Poland	**Полша** [Polsha]
Portugal	**Португалия** [Portougaliya]
Romania	**Румъния** [Roumuniya]
Russia	**Русия** [Rousiya]
Scotland	**Шотландия** [Shotlandiya]
Serbia	**Сърбия** [Surbiya]
Slovakia	**Словакия** [Slovakiya]
Spain	**Испания** [Ispanuya]
Switzerland	**Швейцария** [Shveytsariya]
Turkey	**Турция** [Tourtsiya]
Wales	**Уелс** [Ouels]

I am …
(Аз) съм … [(Az) sum …]

American	**американец** [amerikanets]
Australian	**австралиец** [avstraliets]
Canadian	**канадец** [kanadets]
English	**англичанин** [anglichanin]

Other Nationalities

Albanian	**албанец** [albanets]
Austrian	**австриец** [avstriets]
British	**британец** [britanets]
Bulgarian	**българин** [bulgarin]
Croat	**хърватин** [hutvatin]
Czech	**чех** [cheh]
Dutch	**холандец** [holandets]
French	**французин** [frantsouzin]
German	**немец** [nemets]
Greek	**грък** [gruk]
Hungarian	**унгарец** [oungarets]
Irish	**ирландец** [irlandets]
Italian	**италианец** [italianets]
Polish	**поляк** [polyak]
Portuguese	**португалец** [portougalets]
Romanian	**румънец** [roumunets]
Russian	**руснак** [rousnak]
Scottish	**шотландски** [shotlandski]
Serb	**сърбин** [surbin]
Slovak	**словак** [slovak]
Spanish	**испанец** [ispanets]
Swiss	**швейцарец** [shveytsarets]
Turkish	**турчин** [tourchin]
Welsh	**уелски** [ouelski]

I am a …
(Аз) съм … [(Az) sum …]

businessperson	**бизнесмен** [biznesmen]
computer programmer	**програмист** [programist]
doctor	**доктор** [doktor]
engineer	**инженер** [inzhener]
journalist	**журналист** [zhournalist]
lawyer	**адвокат** [advokat]
librarian	**библиотекар** [bibliotekar]
musician	**музикант** [mouzikant]
police officer	**полицай** [politsay]
salesperson	**продавач** [prodavach]
scientist	**научен работник** [naouchen rabotnik]
secretary	**секретар|ка** [sekretar|ka]
soldier	**войник** [voynik]
student	**студент** [student]
teacher	**учител** [ouchitel]
travel agent	**туристически агент** [touristicheski agent]
waiter/waitress	**сервитьор|ка** [servityor|ka]

I study …
(Аз) следвам … [(Az) sledvam …]

art	**изкуство** [izkoustvo]
biology	**биология** [biologiya]
business	**икономика** [ikonomika]
history	**история** [istoriya]
law	**право** [pravo]
literature	**литература** [literatoura]
medicine	**медицина** [meditsina]
music	**музика** [mouzika]

psychology	**психология** [psihologiya]
theater	**театър** [teatur]

This is my …
Това е … [Tova e …]

mother	**моята майка** [moyata mayka]
father	**моят баща** [moyat bashta]
sister	**моята сестра** [moyata sestra]
brother	**моят брат** [moyat brat]
son	**моят син** [moyat sin]
daughter	**моята дъщеря** [moyata dushterya]
husband	**моят съпруг** [moyat suproug]
wife	**моята съпруга** [moyata suprouga]
grandmother	**моята баба** [moyata baba]
grandfather	**моят дядо** [moyat dyado]
uncle	**моят чичо** [moyat chicho]
aunt	**моята леля** [moyata lelya]
cousin	**моят братовчед** [moyat bratovched]
	моята братовчедка [moyata bratovchedka]
boyfriend	**моят приятел** [moyat priyatel]
girlfriend	**моята приятелка** [moyata priyatelka]

Do you have children?
Имате ли деца? [Imate li detsa?]

Are you married?
Женен ли сте? [Zhenen li ste?]
Омъжена ли сте? [Omuzhena li ste?]

I am married.
For a married man:
Аз съм женен. [Az sum zhenen.]
Женен съм. [Zhenen sum.]
For a married woman:
Аз съм омъжена. [Az sum omuzhena.]
Омъжена съм. [Omuzhena sum.]

I am a single man.
Свободен съм. [Svoboden sum.]
Не съм женен. [Ne sum zhenen.]

I am a bachelor.
Аз съм ерген. [Az sum ergen.]
Ерген съм. [Ergen sum.]

I am an unmarried woman.
Аз съм мома. [Az sum moma.]
Мома съм. [Moma sum.]

We are on vacation.
Тук сме на почивка.
[Touk sme na pochivka.]

I am here to study.
Тук следвам. [Touk sledvam]

TRAVEL & TRANSPORTATION

May I ask you?
Мога ли да Ви попитам?
[Moga li da Vi popitam?]

Where are we?
Къде сме? [Kude sme?]

Which bus/streetcar goes to the center of town?
Кой автобус/трамвай отива до центъра на града?
[Koy avtobous/tramvay otiva do chentura na grada?]

Take bus number 5.
Отидете с автобус номер 5.
[Otidete s avtobous nomer 5.]
Вземете автобус номер 5.
[Vzemete avtobus nomer 5.]

I would like to go to the …
(Аз) бих искал|а да отида в …
[(Az) bih iskal|a da otida v …]

town **града** [grada]
store **магазина** [magazina]

Where can I buy tickets to …?
Къде мога да купя билети за …?
[Kude moga da koupya bileti za …?]

one-way ticket
еднопосочен билет [ednoposochen bilet]

round-trip ticket
билет за отиване и връщане
[bilet za otivane i vrushtane]

Where can I find a travel agency?
Къде мога да намеря пътна агенция?
[Kude moga da namerya putna agentsiya?]

Where is the …?
Къде е …? [Kude e … ?]

bus station
спирката на автобуса
[spirkatata na avtobousa]

streetcar station
спирката на трамвая
[spirkata na tramvaya]

subway
метрото [metroto]

subway station
спирката на метрото
[spirkata na metroto]

train station
гарата [garata]

What is the name of this street?
Как се казва тази улица?
[Kak se kazva tazi oulista?]

Show me on the map, please.
Покажете ми на картата, моля.
[Pokazhete mi na kartata, molya.]

Customs

Border control.
Гранична контрола.
[Granichna kontrola.]

Customs examination.
Митническа проверка.
[Mitnicheska proverka.]

Please show your passport/visa.
Моля, покажете ми Вашия паспорт/ виза.
[Molya, pokazhete mi Vashiya pasport/ viza.]

Here is my passport/visa.
Моля, заповядайте моя паспорт/виза.
[Molya, zapovyadayte moya pasport/viza.]

I am on vacation.
Аз съм на почивка. [Az sum na pochivka.]
На почивка съм. [Na pochivka sum.]

I am a student.
Аз съм студент|ка. [Az sum student|ka.]
Студент|ка съм. [Stoudent|ka sum.]

I will stay for two/four days.
(Аз) ще остана два/четири дена.
[(Az] she ostana dva/chetiri dena.]

I will stay for a week/month.
(Аз) ще остана една седмица/един месец.
[(Az] she ostana edna sedmitsa/edin mesets.]

Do you have anything to declare?
Имате ли нещо за деклариране?
[Imate li neshto za deklarirane?]

I'd like to declare this.
(Аз) Бих искал|а да декларирам това.
[(Az) Bih iskal|a da deklariram tova.]

I've got nothing to declare.
Нямам нищо за деклариране.
[Nyamam nishto za deklarirane.]

Open your bag, please.
Отворете, моля, Вашата/твоята чанта.
[Otvorete, molya, Vashata/tvoyatat chanta.]

Whose is this suitcase?
Чий е този куфар? [Chiy e tozi koufar ?]

What do you have in this bag?
Какво имате в тази чанта?
[Kakvo imate v tazi chanta?]

Here is my luggage.
Това е моят багаж. [Tova e moyat bagazh.]

Shall I open it?
Трябва ли да го отворя?
[Tryabva li da go otvorya?]

May I close it?
Мога ли да го затворя?
[Moga li da go zatvorya?]

This is all I have.
Това е всичко, което имам.
[Tova e vsichko, koeto imam.]

These are gifts.
Това са подаръци. [Tova sa podarusti.]

All these are my clothes. /
All these clothes are mine.
Всичко това са мои дрехи/мое облекло.
[Vsichko tova sa moi drehi/moe obleklo.]

This bag contains only books.
Тази чанта съдържа само книги.
[Tazi chanta sudurzha samo knigi.]

Do I have to pay duty?
Трябва ли да платя мито?
[Tryabva li da platya mito?]

Travel by Plane

Where is the airport?
Къде е летището? [Kude e letishteto?]

Which bus goes to the airport?
Кой автобус отива на летището?
[Koj avtobous otiva na letishteto?]

How far is it?
Колко е далеч? [Kolko e dalech?]

Can you book me for Monday?
Можете ли да ми направите резервация за понеделник?
[Mozhete li da mi napravite rezervatsiya za ponedelnik?]

I would like …
(Аз) бих искал|а … [(Az) bih iskal|a …]

a first-class seat
място в първа класа
[myasto v purva klasa]

a business-class seat
място в бизнес класа
[myasto v biznes klasa]

a coach/economy-class seat
място в икономическа класа
[myasto v ikonomicheska klasa]

Your flight is delayed.
Вашият полет има закъснение.
[Vashiyat polet ima zakusnenie.]

Your flight has been canceled.
Вашият полет беше анулиран.
[Vashiyat polet beshe anouliran.]

That flight is full.
Самолетът е пълен.
[Samoletut e pulen.]

I have lost my bag. Please help me.
Загубила ми се е чантата. Моля, помогнете ми.
[Zagoubila mi se e chantata. Molya, pomognete mi.]

I have lost my ticket.
Загубих самолетния си билет.
[Zagoubih samoletniya si bilet.]

I have missed my flight!
Изпуснах самолета!
[Izpousnah samoleta!]

I would like …
(Аз) бих искал|а … [(Az) bih iskal|a …]

something to drink
нещо за пиене [neshto za piene]

something to eat
нещо за ядене [neshto za yadene]

some coffee
малко кафе [malko kafe]

tea	**чай** [chay]
a newspaper	**вестник** [vestnik]
a magazine	**списание** [spisanie]
some water	**вода** [voda]

airport	**летище** [letishte]
arrival	**пристигане** [pristigane]
departure	**заминаване**[zaminavane], **отлитане** [otlitane]
boarding pass	**бордна карта** [bordna karta]
flight	**полет** [polet]
gate	**изход** [izhod]; **врата** [vrata]
terminal	**терминал** [terminal]
entrance	**вход** [vhod]
exit	**изход** [izhod]
no entry	**влизането забранено** [vlizaneto zabraneno]
no smoking	**пушенето забранено** [pousheneto zabraneno]

Travel by Bus and Streetcar

Where can I get a bus/streetcar schedule?
Къде мога да получа разписанието на автобуса/трамвая?
[Kude moga da poloucha razpisanieto na avtobousa/tramvaya?]

Where can I get a bus/streetcar map?
Къде мога да получа картата на автобуса/трамвая?
[Kude moga da poloucha kartata na avtobousa/tramvaya?]

Where is the nearest bus/streetcar station?
Къде е най-близката спирка на автобуса/трамвая?
[Kude e naj-blizkata spirka na avtobousa/tramvaya?]

Where does the bus/streetcar stop?
Къде спира автобусът/трамваят?
[Kude spira avtobousut/tramvayat?]

Does this bus/streetcar go to the theater?
Този автобус/трамвай отива ли до театъра?
[Tozi avtobous/tramvay otiva li do teatura?]

When is the next bus/streetcar?
Кога е следващият автобус/трамвай?
[Koga e sledvashtiyat avtobous/tramvay?]

Where can I buy a ticket?
Къде мога да си купя билет?
[Kude moga da si koupya bilet?]

How much is the ticket?
Колко струва билетът?
[Kolko strouva biletut?]

driver	**шофьор** [shofyor]
fare	**цената на билет** [tsenata na bilet]
number	**номер** [nomer]
schedule	**разписание** [razpisanie]
station	**станция** [stantsiya]
stop	**спирка** [spirka]
ticket	**билет** [bilet]
transfer	**смяна** [smyana], **прехвърляне** [prehvurlyane]

Travel by Subway

conductor	**кондуктор** [kondouktor]
emergency brake	**аварийна спирачка** [avariyna spirachka]
fine, penalty	**глоба** [globa]
subway map	**карта, план на метрото** [karta, plan na metroto]
subway station	**станция на метрото** [stantsiya na metroto]
subway stop	**спирка на метрото** [spirka na metroto]
token	**жетон** [zheton]

METRO SOFIA
МЕТРО СОФИЯ

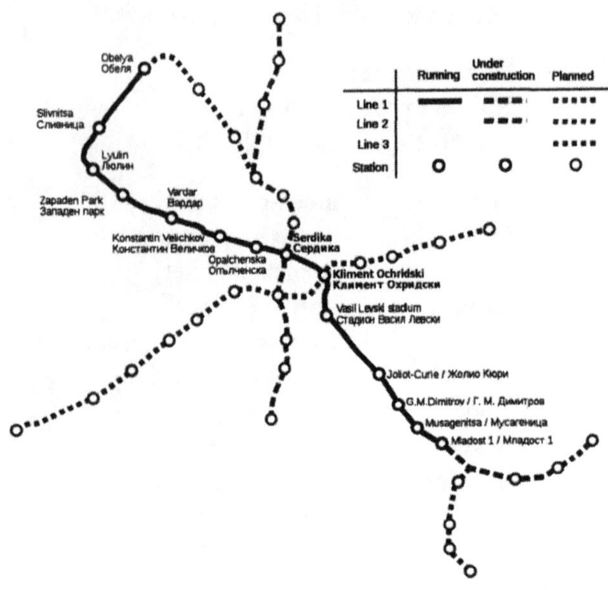

Travel by Train

Which train goes to …?
Кой влак отива до …?
[Koy vlak otiva do …?]

Which platform?
Кой перон? [Koy peron?]

At what time?
В колко часа? [V kolko chasa?]

Travel by Taxi

Where can I get a taxi?
Къде мога да хвана такси?
[Kude moga da hvana taksi?]

Call a taxi for me, please.
Викнете такси за мен, моля.
[Viknete taksi za men, molya.]
Поръчайте ми такси, моля.
[Poruchayte mi taksi, molya.]

Are you free?
Свободен|а ли сте? [Svoboden|a li ste?]

Please stop here.
Моля, спрете тук. [Molya, sprete touk.]

Can you wait here, please?
Можете ли да почакате тук, моля?
[Mozhete li da pochakate touk, molya?]

How much does it cost?
Колко струва? [Kolko strouva?]

Would you take me …?
Бихте ли ме закарал|а …?
[Bihte li me zakaral|a …?]

to the airport
на летището [na letishteto]

to the downtown
до центъра на града
[do tsentura na grada]

to the hotel
до хотела [do hotela]

to the train station
на гарата [na garata]

bicycle	**колело** [kolelo]
bus stop	**спирка на автобуса** [spirka na avtobousa]
car	**автомобил** [avtomobil], **кола** [kola]
road	**път** [put]
station	**спирка** [spirka]
train	**влак** [vlak]
train station	**гара** [gara]

Travel by Car

In the Republic of Bulgaria, kilometers are used instead of miles (1 mile = 1.6 kilometers). Foreigners should preferably have an international driver's license. Speed limits are 50 km/h (31.25 m/h) in towns, 80 km/h (50 m/h) on main roads, and 120 km/h (75 m/h) on divided highways. First-class roads are in good condition and roadside assistance is available. When you enter Bulgaria you buy a vignette at the border, which entitles you to drive on all roads. Highway signs are green, main road and city signs are blue. Yellow fields mean no parking, blue fields mean limited parking with visible parking disk behind the windshield.

Vehicles on the roundabout or coming from the right on unmarked crossings have right of way. Seat belts are required for all passengers. Special attention is required when driving among streetcars in historic city centers, on rural roads where farm animals or slowly moving carts are common, or at night.

I have an international driver's license.
(Аз) имам международна шофьорска книжка.
[(Az) imam mezhdunarodna shofyorska knizhka.]

Where can I rent …?
Къде мога да взема под наем …?
[Kude moga da vzema nod naem …?]

a bicycle	**колело** [kolelo]
a car	**кола** [kola]
a motorcycle	**мотор** [motor]

How much is it …?
Колко струва …? [Kolko struva …?]

per day	**на ден** [na den]
per week	**на седмица** [na sedmitsa]
for two days	**за два дена** [za dva dena]
for five days	**за пет дни**[za pet dni]

Where is the nearest gas station?
Къде е най-близката бензиностанция?
[Kude e nay blizkata benzinostantsiya?]

Full, please.
Моля, пълен резервоар.
[Molya, pulen rezervoar.]

Check …, please.
Проверете …, моля.
[Proverete …, molya.]

the battery **акумулатора** [akoumoulatora]
the brake fluid **спирачната течност** [spirachnata technost]
the oil **маслото** [masloto]
the water **водата** [vodata]

driver's license **шофьорска книжка** [shofyorska knizhka]
insurance policy **застраховка** [zastrahovka]
the car papers **документите за колата** [dokoumentite za kolata]
front seat **предна седалка** [predna sedalka]
back seat **задна седалка** [zadna sedalka]

Asking for Directions

Where is the …?
Къде е …? [Kude e …?]

airport **летището** [letishteto]
art gallery **художествената галерия** [houdozhestvenata galeriya]

bank	**банката** [bankata]
church	**църквата** [tsurkvata]
downtown	**центърът на града** [tsenturut na grada]
market	**пазарът** [pazarut]
station	**станцията**[stantsiyata], **спирката** [spirkata]

Can you show me the route on the map?
Можете ли да ми покажете пътя на картата?
[Mozhete li da mi pokazhete putya na kartata?]

How many kilometers is it to Sofia?
Колко километра е до София?
[Kolko kilometra e do Sofiya?]

Is there a divided highway?
Има ли аутобан?
[Ima li aoutoban?]

What's the name of this street?
Как се казва тази улица?
[Kak se kazva tazi oulitsa?]

Where can I find this address?
Къде мога да намеря този адрес?
[Kude moga da namerya tozi adres?]

It is near.	**Близо е.** [Blizo e.]
Is it near?	**Близо ли е?** [Blizo li e?]
It is far.	**Далеч е.** [Dalech e.]
Is it far?	**Далеч ли е?** [Dalech li e?]

How far is it? **Колко е далеч?** [Kolko e dalech?]

Can I park here?
Мога ли да паркирам тук?
[Moga li da parkiram touk?]

How do I get to …?
Как да стигна до …?
[Kak da stigna do …?]

I want to get to …
(Аз) искам да стигна до …
[(Az) iskam da stigna do …]

Turn left. **Завийте наляво.** [Zaviyte nalyavo.]
Turn right. **Завийте надясно.** [Zaviyte nadyasno.]

behind **зад** [zad]
in front **пред** [pred]

corner **ъгъл** [ugul]

far **далеч** [dalech]
near **близо** [blizo]

right **надясно** [nadyasno]
left **наляво** [nalyavo]

north **север** [sever]
south **юг** [yug]
east **изток** [iztok]
west **запад** [zapad]

parking **паркинг** [parking]
stop **спирам** [spiram]

MONEY

The official currency in the Republic of Bulgaria is the Bulgarian *lev* **(лев)**, which is divided into one hundred *stotinki* **(стотинка)**.

Where is the nearest bank?
Къде е най-близката банка?
[Kude e nay-blizkata banka?]

Where can I change money?
Къде мога да сменя пари?
[Kude moga da smenya pari?]

What is the exchange rate?
Какъв е курсът?
[Kakuv e koursut?]

What's the present rate of exchange for the U.S. dollar to the Bulgarian lev?
Какъв е днешният курс на американския долар към българския лев?
[Kakuv e dneshniyat kours na americanskiya dolar kum bulgarskiya lev?]

I want to open a savings/checking account.
(Аз) бих искал|а да отворя спестовен/ разплащателен влог.
[(Az) bih iskal|a da otvorya spestoven/ razplashtatelen vlog.]

borrow	**взимам пари на заем** [vzimam pari na zaem]
cash	**пари в брой** [pari v broi]
change	**смяна** [smyana]

coins	**монети** [moneti], **дребни пари** [drebni pari]
exchange	**обмяна** [obmyana]
money	**пари** [pari]
return	**връщам** [vrushtam]
signature	**подпис** [podpis]

COMMUNICATIONS

Where can I phone from?
Къде мога да телефонирам?
[Kude moga da telefoniram?]

May I phone from here?
Мога ли да телефонирам от тука?
[Moga li da telefoniram ot touka?]

Where is the nearest public phone?
Къде е най-близката телефонна будка?
[Kude e nay-blizkata telefonna boudka?]

Where is the telephone?
Къде е телефона?
[Kude e telefona?]

I want to make a local call.
(Аз) искам да проведа градски разговор.
[(Az) iskam da proveda gradski razgovor.]

I want to make an international/long-distance call.
Иъкам да проведа международен/ извънградски разговор.
[Iskam da proveda mezdounaroden/ izvungradski razgovor.]

Do you have a telephone directory?
Имате ли телефонен указател?
[Imate li telefonen oukazatel?]

My phone number is …
Моят телефонен номер е …
[Moyat telefonen nomer e …]

How much does it cost?
Колко струва? [Kolko strouva?]

It is … leva.
Струва … лева. [Strouva … leva.]

Hello.
Ало. [Alo.]

This is Iliya speaking.
Илия се обажда. [Iliya se obazhda.]

Can I leave a message?
Мога ли да оставя съобщение?
[Moga li da ostavya suobshtenie?]

I will call again.
(Аз) ще се обадя отново.
[(Az) shte se obadya otnovo.]

I will try again.
(Аз) ще опитам отново.
[(Az) shte opitam otnovo.]

Ask him/her to call this phone number.
Помолете го/я да набере този телефонен номер.
[Pomolete go/ya da nabere tozi telefonen nomer.]

There is a call for you.
Има обаждане за Вас/теб.
[Ima obazhdane za Vas/teb.]

Faxing

I wish to send a fax.
(Аз) искам да изпратя факс.
[(Az) iskam da izpratya faks.]

Can I send/receive faxes here?
Мога ли да изпратя/получа факс тук?
[Moga li da izpratya/poloucha faks touk?]

What is your fax number?
Какъв е вашият номер на факса?
[Kakuv e vashiyat nomer na faksa?]

How much is it per page?
Колко струва за една страница?
[Kolko strouva za edna stranitsa?]

Post Office

Where is the nearest post office?
Къде е най-близката поща?
[Kude e nay-blizkaata poshta?]

Where is the main post office?
Къде е главната поща?
[Kude e glavnata poshta?]

I would like to send …
(Аз) бих искал|а да изпратя …
[(Az) bih iskal|a da izpratya …]

a parcel	**колет** [kolet]
a postcard	**картичка** [kartichka]
a telegram	**телеграма** [telegrama]

I would like to send this letter …
(Аз) бих искал|а да изпратя това писмо …
[(Az) bih iskal|a da izpratya tova pismo …]

by registered mail
препоръчано [preporuchano]

express delivery
с експресна поща [s ekspresna poshta]

by airmail
по въздуха [po vuzdouha]

I am looking for a mailbox.
Търся пощенска кутия.
[Tursya poshtenska koutiya.]

I want to buy stamps.
(Аз) искам да купя марки.
[(Az) iskam da koupya marki.]

How many stamps do I need?
Колко марки са необходими?
[Kolko marki sa neobhodimi?]

Give me …, please.
Дайте ми …, моля.
[Dayte mi …, molya.]

one stamp	**една марка**	[edna marka]
two stamps	**две марки**	[dve marki]
five stamps	**пет марки**	[pet marki]

Internet Service

I am looking for an Internet access point.
(Аз) търся точка за достъп до Интернет.
[(Az) tursya tochka za dostup do Internet.]

I am looking for a WiFi connection.
(Аз) търся WiFi връзка.
[(Az) tursya WiFi vruzka.]

Is there an Internet café in town?
Има ли в града интернет кафе?
[Ima li v graada internet kafe?]

I want to send an e-mail to my friend.
(Аз) бих искал|а да изпратя е-майл на своят|а приятел|ка.
[(Az) bih iskal|a da izpratya e-mail na svoyat|a priyatel|ka.]

How much does it cost to use the Internet?
Колко струва използването на интернет?
[Kolko strouva izpolzvaneto na internet?]

computer	**компютър** [kompyutur]
e-mail	**и-мейл**[i-meyl], **електронна поща** [elektronna poshta]
enter	**влизам** [vlizam]
letter	**писмо** [pismo]
number	**число** [chislo]
password	**парола** [parola]
postcard	**картичка** [kartichka]
stamp	**марка** [marka]

ACCOMMODATIONS

I am looking for a furnished/unfurnished apartment.
(Аз) търся обзаведен/необзаведен апартамент.
[(Az) tursya obzaveden/neobzaveden apartament.]

How much is it …?
Колко струва …?
[Kolko strouva …?]

per month **месечно** [mesechno]
per week **седмично** [sedmichno]

Is heat/water/electricity included?
Отоплението/водата/токът включени ли са?
[Otoplenieto/vodata/tokut vklyucheni li sa?]

Where do I pay for water and electricity?
Къде се плаща за вода и електричество?
[Kude se plashta za voda i elektrichestvo?]

Hotels

I am looking for …
(Аз) търся … [(Az) tursya …]

a good hotel **добър хотел** [dobur hotel]
an inexpensive hotel **евтин хотел** [evtin hotel]

How much is it per room?
Колко струва една стая?
[Kolko strouva edna staya?]

Is it with breakfast included?
Закуската влиза ли в цената?
[Zakouskata vliza li v tsenata?]

I would like …
(Аз) бих искал|а … [(Az) bih iskal|a …]

a single room	**единична стая** [edinichna staya]
a double room	**двойна стая** [dvoyna staya]

We would like …
Бихме искали … [Bihme iskali …]

a room	**стая** [staya]
two rooms	**две стаи** [dve stai]

It costs … per night.
Струва … на нощ.
[Strouva … na nosht.]

I want a room with …
(Аз) искам стая с …
[(Az) iskam staya s …]

a bathroom	**баня** [banya]
a shower	**душ** [doush]
a telephone	**телефон** [telefon]
a television	**телевизор** [televizor]

I will stay for …
(Аз) ще остана … [(Az) she ostana…]

one day	**един ден** [edin den]
two days	**два дни** [dva dni]
five days	**пет дена** [pet dena]

My name is …
Казвам се … [Kazbam se …]
Името ми е … [Imeto mi e …]

I would like to get my bill.
(Аз) бих искал|а да получа сметката.
[(Az) bih iskal|a da polucha smetkata.]

Can I pay with …?
Мога ли да платя …?
[Moga li da playa …?]

a check	**с чек** [s chek]
a credit card	**с кредитна карта** [s kreditna karta]

Please, bring me …
Моля, донесете ми …
[Molya, donesete mi …]

a glass	**чаша** [chasha]
a pillow	**възглавница** [vuzglavnitsa]
soap	**сапун** [sapoun]
a towel	**кърпа за ръце** [kurpa za rutse]

Please, bring me some …
Моля, донесете ми малко …
[Molya, donesete mi malko …]

juice	**сок** [sok]
water	**вода** [voda]

Can I wash these clothes?
Мога ли да изпера тези дрехи?
[Moga li da izpera tezi drehi?]

I am in room number 9 (nine).
(Аз) съм в стая номер 9 (девет).
[(Az) sum v staya nomer 9 (devet).]

bathroom	**баня** [banya]
bed	**легло** [leglo]
bill	**сметка** [smetka]
blanket	**одеало** [odealo]
double bed	**двойно легло** [dvoyno leglo]
electricity	**електричество** [elektrichestvo]
ice	**лед** [led]
key	**ключ** [klyuch]
linen	**чаршафи** [charshafi]
mattress	**матраци** [matratsi]
mirror	**огледало** [ogledalo]
pillow	**възглавница** [vuzglavnitsa]
refrigerator	**хладилник** [hladilnik]
restroom	**тоалетна** [toaletna], **WC** [WC]
room	**стая** [staya]
shower	**душ** [doush]
suitcase	**куфар** [koufar]
towel	**кърпа** [kurpa]

water **вода** [voda]
cold water **студена вода** [stoudena voda]
hot water **вряла** [vryala], **гореща вода** [goreshta voda]
warm water **топла вода** [topla voda]

FOOD & DRINK

The Bulgarian national dish is *banitsa*, traditionally prepared with homemade dough layered with a mixture of cheese, yogurt, and eggs and then baked. It can be eaten warm, right from the oven, or cold. Usually *banitsa* is served for breakfast with plain yogurt, *boza*, a slightly sweet fermented drink, or *ayran*, a refreshing drink with yogurt, water, and salt. There are many variations: *banitsa* with spinach (*banitsa sus spanak*), *banitsa* with meat (*banitsa s meso*), and sweet versions like *banitsa* with milk (*mlechna banitsa*), or *banitsa* with pumpkin (*tikvenik*), a New Year's favorite. On Christmas Eve or New Year's Eve a *banitsa* is made with lucky charms hidden in the dough, and each guest hopes to find one in their piece. The lucky charms can be a coin (the grand prize), happy or humorous wishes on small pieces of paper wrapped in foil, or dogwood buds for good health and long life.

breakfast	**закуска** [zakouska]
lunch	**обяд** [obyad]
dinner	**вечеря** [vecherya]
snack	**снек** [snek], **лека закуска** [leka zakouska]
salad	**салата** [salata]

starter/appetizer **предястие** [predyastie], **ордьовър** [ordyovur]
main course **главно ястие** [glavno yastie]
dessert **десерт** [desert]

I am full.
Наял|а съм се. [Nayal|a sum se.]
Стига ми. [Stiga mi.]
Сит/сита съм. [Sit/sita sum.]

I am hungry.
Аз съм гладен|а. [Az sum gladen|a.]
Гладен|а съм. [Gladen|a sum.]

I am thirsty.
Аз съм жаден|а. [Az sum zhaden|a.]
Жаден|а съм. [Zhaden|a sum.]

Waiter! / Waitress!
Сервитьор|ка! [Servityor|ka!]

I would like to make a reservation.
(Аз) бих искал|а да направя резервация.
[(Az) bih iskal|a da napravya rezervatsiya.]
(Аз) бих искал|а да резервирам.
[(Az) bih iskal|a da rezerviram.]

A table for two, please.
Маса за двама, моля.
[Masa za dvama, molya.]

Is this table free?
Тази маса свободна ли е?
[Tazi masa svobodna li e?]

Are there free seats?
Има ли свободни места?
[Ima li svobodni mesta?]

The menu, please.
Менюто, моля. [Menyuto, molya.]

Wine list, please.
Листа с напитките, моля.
[Lista s napitkite, molya.]

We'd like to order.
Бихме искали да поръчаме.
[Bihme iskali da poruchame.]

Can you recommend something to us?
Можете ли да ни препоръчате нещо?
[Mozhete li da ni preporuchate neshto?]

Do you have a children's menu?
Имате ли детско меню?
[Imate li detsko menyu?]

I'd like …
(Аз) бих искал|а …
[(Az) bih iskal|a …]

I am a vegetarian.
Аз съм вегетарианец/вегетарианка.
[Az sum vegetarianets/vegetarianka.]
Вегетарианец/вегетарианка съм.
[Vegetarianets/vegetarianka sum.]

Is this …?
Това … ли е? [Tova … li e?]

vegetarian	**вегетарианско** [vegetariansko]
kosher	**кошер** [kosher]
halal	**халал** [halal]

What would you like to drink?
Какво ще пиете?
[Kakvo shte piete?]

I didn't order this.
Не съм поръчал|а това.
[Ne sum poruchal|a tova.]

It was delicious.
Беше вкусно. [Beshe vkusno.]

This is overcooked/undercooked.
Това е преварено, препечено/ недоварено, недопечено.
[Tova e prevareno, prepecheno/ nedovareno, nedopecheno.]

This is not hot/cold.
Това не е топло/студено.
[Tova ne e toplo/studeno.]

Where is the restroom, please?
Къде е тоалетната, моля?
[Kude e toaletnata, molya?]

Can I have the bill?
Мога ли да получа сметката?
[Moga li da polouсha smetkata?]

The bill, please.
Сметката, моля. [Smetkata, molya.]

Here is your bill, please.
Ето Вашата сметка, моля.
[Eto Vashata smetka, molya.]

Here is your tip.
Ето Вашият бакшиш.
[Eto Vashiyat bakshish.]

I think the bill is incorrect.
(Аз) мисля, че сметката не отговаря.
[(Az) mislya, che smetkata ne otgovarya.]

Could you pass me …?
Можете ли да ми подадете …?
[Mozhete li da mi podadete …?]

an ashtray	**един пепелник** [edin pepelnik]
the bread	**хляба** [hlyaba]
a cup	**една чаша** [edna chasha]
a fork	**една вилица** [edna vilitsa]
a glass	**стъклена чаша** [stuklena chasha]
a knife	**един нож** [edin nozh]
a napkin	**една салфетка** [edna salfetka]
the pepper	**пипера** [pipera]
the salt	**солта** [solta]
a spoon	**супена лъжица** [soupena luzhitsa]
the sugar	**захарта** [zahar]

I would like …
(Аз) бих искал|а … [(Az) bih iskal|a …]

beer	**бира** [bira]
dark	**тъмна** [tumna]
light	**светла** [svetla]
draught	**наливна** [nalivna]
Pilsner	**пилзенска** [pilzner]
cocoa	**какао** [kakao]
coffee	**кафе** [kafe]
juice	**сок** [sok]
milk	**мляко** [mlyako]
tea	**чай** [chay]
water	**вода** [voda]

Fruits

apple	**ябълка** [yabulka]
apricot	**кайсия** [kaysiya]
banana	**банан** [banan]
grapes	**грозде** [grozde]
lemon	**лимон** [limon]
plum	**слива** [sliva]
peach	**праскова** [praskova]

Vegetables

beans	**фасул** [fasoul]
cabbage	**зеле** [zele]
carrot	**морков** [morkov]
cucumber	**краставица** [krastavitsa]
green beans	**зелен фасул** [zelen fasul]
green peas	**зелен грах** [zelen grah]

lentils	**леща** [leshta]
mushroom	**гъба** [guba]
onion	**лук** [louk]
potatoes	**картофи** [kartofi]
spinach	**спанак** [spanak]
tomato	**домат** [domat]

Dairy

butter	**масло** [maslo]
cream	**сметана** [smetana]
ice-cream	**сладолед** [sladoled]
milk	**мляко** [mlyako]
yogurt	**кисело мляко** [kiselo mlyako]

cheeses

сирене [sirene] (*traditional white brine Bulgarian cheese, best from sheep's milk*)

кашкавал [kashkaval] (*traditional Bulgarian cheese, best from sheep's milk*)

Proteins

beef	**говеждо месо** [govezhdo meso]
burger	**бургер** [bourger]
chicken	**пиле** [pile]
cutlet	**шницел** [shnitsel]
duck	**патица** [patitsa]
eggs	**яйца** [yaytsa]
fish	**риба** [riba]

ground meat	**мляно месо** [meso], **кайма** [kayma]
ham	**шунка** [shounka]
lamb chop	**агнешки котлет** [agneshki kotlet]
meatball	**кюфте** [kyufte]
mutton	**овнешко месо** [ovneshko meso]
pork	**свинско месо** [svinsko meso]
sausage	**наденица** [nadenitsa]
steak	**пържола** [purzhola]
veal	**телешко месо** [teleshko meso]

SHOPPING

When do the shops open/close?
В колко часа отварят/затварят магазините?
[V kolko chasa otvaryat/zatvaryat magazinite?]

I want to go shopping.
(Аз) искам да пазарувам.
[(Az) iskam da pazarouvam.]

Where can I buy ...?
Къде мога да купя ...?
[Kude moga da koupya …?]

Can you take me to the shopping mall?
Можете ли да ме закарате до универсалния магазин?
[Mozhe li da me zakarate do ouniversal-niya magazin?]

I need some things.
Аз се нуждая от някои неща.
[Az se nouzhdaya ot nyakoi neshta.]
Нуждая се от някои неща.
[Nouzhdaya se ot nyakoi neshta.]

Please, wrap this for me.
Моля, опаковайте ми го.
[Molya, opakovayte mi go.]

How much does it cost?
Колко струва? [Kolko strouva?]

Where do I pay?
Къде мога да платя?
[Kude moga da platya?]

Stores

Where can I find a …?
Къде мога да намеря …?
[Kude moga da namerya …?]

bakery	**пекарница** [pekarnitsa]
bookstore	**книжарница** [knizharnitsa]
butcher	**месарница** [mesarnitsa], **касапница** [kasapnitsa]
clothing store	**магазин за дрехи** [magazin za drehi]
drugstore	**дрогерия** [drogeriya]
florist	**цветарница** [tsvetarnitsa]
fruit store	**магазин за плодове** [magazin za plodove]
grocery store	**бакалница** [bakalnitsa]
market	**пазар** [pazar]
music store	**музикален магазин** [muzikalen magazin]
pharmacy	**аптека** [apteka]
spice shop	**магазин за подправки** [magazin za podpravki]
shoemaker	**обущар** [oboushtar]
supermarket	**супермаркет** [soupermarket]
tailor	**шивач|ка** [shivach|ka]
watchmaker	**часовникар** [chasovnikar]

Clothing

What are you looking for?
Какво търсите? [Kakvo tursite?]

Where can I get …?
Къде мога да намеря …?
[Kude moga da namerya …?]

May I try this one?
Мога ли да го пробвам?
[Moga li da go probvam?]

Does it fit me?
По мярка ли ми е? [Po myarka li mi e?]
Става ли ми? [Stava li mi?]

It's too expensive.
Много е скъпо. [Mnogo e skupo.]

bigger	**по-голямо** [po-golyamo]
smaller	**по-малко** [po-malko]
shorter	**по-късо** [po-kuso]
longer	**по-дълго** [po-dulgo]
cheaper	**по-евтино** [po-evtino]
more expensive	**по-скъпо** [po-skupo]
women's size	**дамска големина** [damska golemina]
men's size	**мъжка големина** [muzhska golemina]
children's size	**детска големина** [detska golemina]

I want to buy a …
(Аз) искам да купя …
[(Az} iskam da koupya …]

blouse	**блуза** [blouza]
bag	**чанта** [chanta]
coat	**палто** [palto]
dress	**рокля** [roklya]
handkerchief	**носна кърпа** [nosna kurpa]
hat	**шапка** [shapka]
nightgown	**пеньоар** [penyoar]
pajamas	**пижама** [pizhama]
shirt	**риза** [riza]
shoes	**обувки** [obouvki]
skirt	**пола** [pola]
socks	**къси чорапи** [kusi chorapi]
suit	**костюм** [kostyum]

cashmere	**кашмир** [kashmir]
cotton	**памук** [pamouk]
denim	**деним** [denim]
leather	**кожа** [kozha]
linen	**лен** [len]
silk	**коприна** [koprina]
wool	**вълна** [vulna]

Drugstore

antibiotic	**антибиотик** [antibiotik]
band-aid	**превръзка** [prevruzka]
batteries	**батерии** [baterii]
comb	**гребен** [greben]
conditioner	**балсам за коса** [balsam za kosa]

condom	**презерватив** [prezervativ]
diaper(s)	**памперси** [pampersi], **пелени** [peleni]
hairbrush	**четка за коса** [chetka za kosa]
lipstick	**червило** [chervilo]
lotion	**мазило** [mazilo], **крем** [krem]
painkiller	**лекарство срещу болка** [lekarstvo sreshtou bolka]
powder	**пуудра** [poudra]
razor	**самобръсначка** [samobrusnachka]
shampoo	**шампоан** [shampoan]
soap	**сапун** [sapoun]
tampons	**тампони** [tamponi]
tissue	**салфетки** [salfetki], **книжни кърпички** [knizhni kurpichki]
toothbrush	**четка за зъби** [chetka za zubi]
toothpaste	**паста за зъби** [pasta za zubi]

Bookstore

Where can I find a bookstore?
Къде мога да намеря книжарница?
[Kude moga da namerya knizharnitsa?]

Is there a bookstore nearby?
Има ли книжарница наблизо?
[Ima li knizharnitsa nablizo?]

Do you have …?
Имате ли, моля, …?
[Imate li, molya, …?]

a dictionary	**речник** [rechnik]
English books	**английски книги** [angliyski knigi]
a guide of Sofia	**пътеводител за София** [putevoditel za Sofiya]
a map	**карта** [karta]
a novel	**роман** [roman]

I want to buy …
(Аз) искам да купя …
[(Az) iskam da koupya …]

a book	**книга** [kniga]
a magazine	**списание** [spisanie]
a newspaper	**вестник** [vestnik]
a notebook	**тефтерче** [tefterche]
a pen	**химикалка** [himikalka]
a pencil	**молив** [moliv]

Camera Store

I'd like … film for this camera.
(Аз) бих искал|а … филм за този апарат.
[(Az) bih iskal|a … film za tozi aparat.]

black and white	**черно-бял** [cherno-byal]
color	**цветен** [tsveten]

How much does it cost?
Колко струва?
[Kolko strouva?]

Could you make prints of the images on this CD?
Можете ли да отпечатате копия от снимките на това CD?
[Mozhete li da otpechatate kopiya ot snimkite na tova CD?]

I'd like a copy of this print.
(Аз) бих искал|а копие от тази снимка.
[(Az) bih iskal|a kopie ot tazi snimka.]

When will the prints be ready?
Кога снимките ще бъдат готови?
[Koga snimkite shte budat gotovi?]

Could you burn them to a CD?
Може ли да ги запишете на CD?
[Mozhe li da gi zapishete na CD?]

Could you put them on this drive?
Може ли да ги запишете на тази карта за памет?
[Mozhe li da gi zapishete na tazi karta za pamet?]

Could you develop this film?
Можете ли да проявите този филм?
[Mozhete li da proyavite tozi film?]

When will the film be ready?
Кога филмът ще бъде готов?
[Koga filmut shte bude gotov?]

battery	**батерия** [bateriya]
CD	**CD, компакт диск** [Si Di, kompakt disk]

charger	**зарядно** [zaryadno]
enlargement	**увеличение** [ouvelichenie]
flash	**светкавица** [svetkavicha]
lens	**обектив** [obektiv]
memory	**памет** [pamet]
memory card	**карта за памет** [karta za pamet]
print	**печатане, принтиране** [pechatane, printirane]
take a picture	**правя снимка** [pravya snimka], **снимам** [snimam]
USB drive / flash drive	**USB / флеш памет** [USB / flesh pamet]

3 in. x 5 in. = 9 cm. x 13 cm.
девет на тринайсет
[devet na trinayset]

4 in. x 6 in. = 10 cm. x 15 cm.
десет на петнайсет
[deset na petnayset]

8 in. x 10 in. = 20 cm. x 25 cm.
двайсет на двайсет и пет
[dvayset na dvayset i pet]

wallet size = 6 cm. x 9 cm.
шест на девет
[shest na devet]

SERVICES

At the Beauty Salon

I would like …
(Аз) бих искал|а … [(Az) bih iskal|a …]

a haircut	**да се подстрижа** [da se podstrizha]
a shave	**бръснене** [brusnene]
a hair wash	**измиване на коса** [izmivane na kosa]
a massage	**масаж** [masazh]
hair spray	**лак за коса** [lak za kosa]

to make an appointment …
да запиша час … [da zapisha chas …]

for tomorrow	**за утре** [za outré]

I want my hair colored/highlighted.
(Аз) бих искал|а да си боядисам/ изсветля косата.
[(Az) bih iskal|a da si boyadisam/izsvetlya kosata.]

I want my hair curled/blow-dried/ straightened.
(Аз) бих искал|а студено къдрене/ сушене/изправяне.
[(Az) bih iskal|a stoudeno kudrene/ soushene/ izpravyane.]

Laundry and Dry Cleaning

Where can I take my clothes to be washed?
Къде мога да изпера дрехите си?
[Kude moga da izpera drehite si?]

Is there a dry cleaner nearby?
Има ли наблизо химическо чистене?
[Ima li nablizo himichesko chistene?]

I would like to wash these clothes.
(Аз) бих искал|а да изпера тези дрехи.
[(Az) bih iskal|a da izpera tezi drehi.]

Please, separate light/dark-colored clothing.
Моля, изперете отделно тъмните/цветните дрехи.
[Molya, izperete otdelno tumnite/tsvetnite drehi.]

Do not wash this dress in …
Не перете тази рокля в …
[Neperete tazi roklya v …]

cold water	**студена вода** [stoudena voda]
hot water	**гореща вода** [goreshta voda]
warm water	**топла вода** [topla voda]

I want to iron …
(Аз) исам да изгладя …
[(Az) iskam da izgladya …]

this dress **тази рокля** [tazi roklya]

this blouse	**тази блуза** [tazi blouza]
this shirt	**тази риза** [tazi riza]

Can you remove this stain?
Може ли да изчистите това петно?
[Mozhe li da izchistite tova petno?]

clothes	**дрехи** [drehi]
	бельо [belyo]
	облекло [obleklo]
detergent	**прах за пране** [prah za prane]
dry cleaner	**химическо чистене** [himichesko chistene]
fabric softener	**омекотител** [omekotitel]
iron	*n.* **ютия** [yutiya]
	v. **гладя** [gladya]
starch	*v.* **колосвам** [kolosvam]
water	**вода** [voda]

CULTURE & ENTERTAINMENT

Where can I find the theater?
Къде се намира театърът?
[Kude se namira teaturut?]

Please, can you show me on the map?
Можете ли да ми покажете на картата, моля?
[Mozhete li da mi pokazhete na kartata, molya?]

I would like to go to the theater.
(Аз) бих искал|а да отида на театър.
[(Az) bih iskal|a da otida na teatur.]

Do you have tickets, please?
Имате ли билети, моля?
[Imate li bileti, molya?]

I would like to go to … tonight.
(Аз) бих искал|а да отида … тази вечер.
[(Az) bih iskal|a da otida … tazi vecher.]

the cinema	**на кино** [na kino]
a concert	**на концерт** [na konstert]
the festival	**на фестивала** [na festivala]

How much are the tickets?
Колко струват билетите?
[Kolko strouvat biletite?]

At what time does it start?
В колко часа започва?
[V kolko chasa zapochva?]

How long is the performance?
Колко дълго ще продължи представлението?
[Kolko dulgo shte produlzhi predstavlenieto.]

One ticket for today, please.
Един билет за днес, моля.
[Edin bilet za dnes, molya.]

Two tickets for tonight, please.
Два билета за вечерното представление, моля.
[Dva bileta za vechernoto predstavlenie, molya.]

Five tickets for tomorrow, please.
Пет билета за утре, моля.
[Pet bileta za outre, molya.]

in the front	**отпред** [otpred]
in the middle	**по средата** [po sredata]
in the back	**отзад** [otzad]
orchestra	**оркестър** [orkestur]
mezzanine	**мецанин** [metsanin]
box seat	**ложа** [lozha]

Please, can you show me to my seat?
Моля, можете ли да ми покажете моето място?
[Molya, mozhete li da mi pokazete moeto myasto?]

What kind of music do you like?
Какъв вид музика обичате?
[Kakuv vid muzika obichate?]

I like …
(Аз) обичам … [(Az) obicham …]

chamber music	**камерна музика** [kamerna mouzika]
classical music	**класическа музика** [klasicheska mouzika]
hip hop	**хип-хоп** [hip-hop]
jazz	**джаз** [dzaz]
pop music	**популярна музика** [popoulyarna mouzika]
rock'n'roll	**рокендрол** [rokendrol]

castle	**замък** [zamuk]
cello	**чело** [chelo]
church	**църква** [tsurkva]
cinema	**кино** [kino]
city walk	**разходка из града** [pazhodka iz grada]
comedy	**комедия** [komediya]
dance	**танц** [tants]
drama	**драма** [drama]
drums	**барабани** [barabani]
folk/traditional	**фолклор/традиционен** [folklor/traditsionen]
music	**музика** [mouzika]
organ	**орган** [organ]
performance	**представление** [predstavlenie]

piano	**пиано** [piano]
play	**пиеса** [piesa]
row	**ред** [red]
seat	**място** [myesto]
ticket	**билет** [bilet]
trumpet	**тромпет** [trompet]
viola	**виола** [viola]
violin	**цигулка** [tsigoulka]

Library

I am looking for a library.
(Аз) търся библиотека.
[(Az) tursya biblioteka.]

Can you show me, please?
Можете ли да ми покажете, моля?
[Mozhete li da mi pokazhete, molya?]

book	**книга** [kniga]
library	**библиотека** [biblioteka]

Museum

art	**изкуство** [izkoustvo]
cafeteria	**кафетерия** [kafeteriya], **ресторант на самообслужване** [restorant na samoobsluzhvane]
coatroom	**гардероб** [garderob]
entry/entrance	**вход** [vhod]
exit	**изход** [izhod]
guide	**пътеводител** [putevoditel]

opening hours **работно време** [rabotno vreme]

discounts

senior discount
намаление за пенсионери
[namalenie za pensioneri]

student discount
намаление за студенти
[namalenie za stoudenti]

youth discount
намаление за младежи
[namalenie za mladezhi]

tickets

adult tickets
билети за възрастни
[bileti za vuzrastni]

children's tickets
билети за деца
[bileti za detsa]

Where is the coatroom?
Къде е гардеробът?
[Kude e garderobut?]

put one's coat in coatroom
давам палтото си на гардероб
[davam paltoto si na garderob]

get one's coat from coatroom
взимам палтото си от гардероба
[vzimam paltoto si ot garderoba]

That's not my coat.
Това не е моето палто.
[Tova ne e moeto palto.]

Sightseeing

art gallery
галерия на изобразителното изкуство
[galeriya na izobraqzitelnoto izkoustvo]

building	**сграда** [sgrada]
cathedral	**катедрала** [katedrala]
exhibition	**изложба** [izlozhba]
fair	**панаир** [panair]
gallery	**галерия** [galeriya]
memorial	**паметник** [pametnik]
museum	**музей** [mouzey]
square	**площад** [ploshtad]
main square	**главен площад** [glaven polshtad]
tour	**обиколка** [obikolka] **разходка** [razhodka] **екскурзия** [ekskourziya]
tour in English	**обиколка на английски език** [obikolka na angliyski ezik]

Can we take photos?
Можем ли да снимаме?
[Mozhem li da snimame?]

Can you take a picture of me?
Можете ли да ми направите снимка?
[Mozhete li da mi napravite snimka?]

SPORTS

What kind of sports do you like?
Какъв вид спорт обичате?
[Kakuv vid sport obichate?]

I would like to play …
(Аз) бих искал|а да играя …
[(Az) bih iskal|a da igraya …]

I would like to watch a game of …
(Аз) бих искал|а да гледам мач по …
[(Az) bih iskal|a da glegam mach po …]

basketball	**баскетбол** [basketbol]
golf	**голф** [golf]
hockey	**хокей** [hokei]
soccer	**футбол** [foutbol]
tennis	**тенис** [tenis]

ball	**топка** [topka]
basketball	**баскетбол** [basketbol]
chess	**шах** [shah]
clock	**часовник** [chasovnik]
coach	**треньор** [trenyor]
game	**игра** [igra]
handball	**хандбал** [handbal]
roller-skates	**летни кънки** [letni kunki]
run	**тичане** [tichane]
skate	**пързаляне на кънки** [purzalyane na kunki]
stadium	**стадион** [stadion]
swim	**плуване** [plouvane]
team	**тим** [tim], **отбор** [otbor]
volleyball	**волейбол** [voleybol]

whistle	**свиря** [svirya]

Hiking, Skiing, Mountaineering

alpine	**алпийски** [alpiyski]
hike	**пешеходен излет** [peshehoden izlet]
hiking tour	**пешеходна екскурзия** [peshehodna ekskourziya]
marked footpath	**туристическа пътека** [touristicheska puteka]
mountain	**планина** [planina]
in the mountains	**на планина** [na planina]
mountaineer	**алпинист** [alpinist]
mountaineering	**алпинизъм** [alpinizum]
peak	**връх** [vruh]
ski	**ски** [ski]
skiing	**пързалям се на ски** [purzalyam se na ski]
ski lift	**влек** [vlek]
sledge	**шейна** [sheyna]
(go) sledging	**пързалям се с шейна** [purzalyam se s sheyna]

Swimming and Boating

Where is the swimming pool?
Къде е басейнът?
[Kude e baseinut?]

boat / ship	**лодка**[lodka]
	кораб [korab]
boater / sailor	**лодкар** [lodkar]
	моряк [moryak]

travel by boat	**пътуване с лодка** [putouvane s lodka]
	пътуване с кораб [putouvane s korab]
river	**река** [reka]
down the river	**по реката** [po rekata]

HEALTH

Medical facilities are available throughout Bulgaria. Doctors and hospitals often expect cash payment for health services. Tourists are advised to have medical insurance that is valid worldwide.

Emergency Numbers

Unified EU emergency	112
Ambulance	150
Fire	160
Police/traffic police	166
Roadside assistance	146

Illness

Please, call an ambulance!
Моля, извикайте бърза помощ!
[Molya, izvikayte burza pomosht!]

I need to see a physician.
Аз се нуждая от лекар.
[Az se nouzhdaya ot lekar.]
Нуждая се от лекар.
[Nouzhdaya se ot lekar.]

Is there a doctor who speaks English?
Тук има ли лекар, който да говори английски?
[Touk ima li lekar, koyto da govori angliyski?]

What is the problem?
Какъв е проблемът?
[Kakuv e problemut?]

I am sick.
Аз съм болен/болна.
[Az sum bolen/bolna.]
Болен/Болна съм.
[Bolen/Bolna sum.]

My friend is sick.
Моят приятел е болен.
[Moyat priyatel e bolen.]
Моята приятелка е болна.
[Moyata priyatelka e bolna.]

How long have you been sick?
Колко дълго сте болен/болна?
[Kolko dulgo ste bolen/bolna?]

Where does it hurt?
Къде Ви/те боли? [Kude Vi/te boli?]

It hurts here.
Тук боли. [Touk boli.]

I have been throwing up.
(Аз) повръщах. [(Az) povrushtah.]

I feel dizzy.
Вие ми се свят. [Vie mi se svyat.]

I cannot eat.
(Аз) не могa да ям.
[(Az) ne moga da yam.]

I cannot sleep.
(Аз) не мога да спя.
[(Az) ne moga da spya.]

I feel better.
Чуствам се по-добре.
[Chouvstvam se po-dobre.]

I feel worse.
Зле ми е. [Zle mi e.]
Чуствам се по-зле.
[Chouvstvsm se po-zle.]

I am tired.
Аз съм изморен|а. [Az sum izmoren|a.]
Изморен|а съм. [Izmoren|a sum.]

I am pregnant.
Аз съм бременна. [Az sum bremenna.]
Бременна съм. [Bremenna sum.]

I am diabetic.
Имам диабет. [Imam diabet.]

I have …
(Аз) имам …
[(Az) imam …]

You have …
Ти имаш …
[Ti imash …]

an allergy	**алергия** [alergiya]
a broken bone	**счупване** [schoupvane] **счупена кост** [schoupena kost]
a cold	**хрема** [hrema]

diarrhea	**разстройство** [razstroystvo]
a fever	**температура** [temperatoura]
	треска [treska]
food poisoning	**хранително отравяне** [hranitelno otravyane]
a heart attack	**сърдечен инфаркт** [surdechen ihfarkt]
	сърдечен пристъп [surdechen pristup]
a sprain	**навяхване** [navyahvane]
	изкълчване [izkulchvane]
a sunburn	**слънчево изгаряне** [slunchevo izgaryane]
sunstroke	**слънчев удар** [slunchev oudar]
	слънчасване [slunchasvsne]
a wound	**рана** [rana]
	нараняване [narahyavane]

I have a cold.
Аз съм настинал|а. [Az cum nastinal|a.]
Настинал|а съм. [Nastinal|a sum.]

I have …
Боли ме ... [Boli me …]
Мене ме боли … [Mene me boli…]

a backache	**гърбът** [gurbut]

an earache	**ухото** [ouhoto]
a headache	**главата** [glavata]
a sore throat	**гърлото** [gurloto]
a stomachache	**стомахът** [stomahut]

I have high blood pressure.
(Аз) имам високо кръвно налягане.
[(Az) imam visokso kruvno nalyagane.]

I have low blood pressure.
(Аз) имам ниско кръвно налягане.
[(Az) imam nisko kruvno nalyagane.]

I am allergic to …
(Аз) имам алергия към …
[(Az) imam alergiya kum …]

anethesia	**анестезия** [anesteziya]
dairy	**млечни продукти** [mlechni produkti]
peanuts	**фъстъци** [fustutsi]
penicillin	**пеницилин** [penitsilin]
shellfish	**миди** [midi]

Take these pills once/twice a day.
Взимайте тези лекарства един път/два пъти на ден.
[Vizmayate tesi lekarstva edin put/dva puti na den.]

You will be fine.
Ще се почувствате по-добре.
[Shte se pochouvstvste po-dobre.]

I'd like to make an appointment with a doctor.
(Аз) бих искал|а да запазя час при лекар.
[(Az) bih iskal|a da zapazya chas pri lekar.]

I have health insurance.
(Аз) имам здравна застраховка.
[(Az) imam zdravna zastrahovka.]

Where is the nearest hospital?
Къде е най-близката болница?
[Kude e hay-blizkata bolnitsa?]

bandage	**превръзка** [prevruzka]
burn	**изгаряне** [izgaryane]
mild	**умерен** [oumeren]
serious	**сериозен** [seriozen]
severe	**тежък** [tezhuk]
emergency room	**реанимация** [reanimatsiya]
medicine	**лекарство** [lekapstvo]
painkiller	**лекарство срещу болка** [lekarstvo sreshtou bolka]
pharmacy	**аптека** [apteka]
prescription	**рецепта** [retsepta]
surgeon	**хирург** [hirourg]

At the Dentist

Could you recommend a good dentist?
Можете ли да ми препоръчате добър зъболекар?
[Mozhete li da mi preporuchate dobur zubolekar?]

I've lost a filling.
Падна ми пломбата.
[Padna mi plombata.]

I have a broken tooth.
(Аз) имам счупен зъб.
[(Az) imam schoupen zub.]
Счупи ми се зъбът.
[Schoupi mi se zubut.]

gums	**венци** [ventsi]
teeth	**зъби** [zubi]
tongue	**език** [ezik]
tooth	**зъб** [zub]
toothache	**болки в зъбите** [bolki v zubite]
	зъбобол [zubobol]

Eyesight

I need glasses.
(Аз) имам нужда от очила. [(Az) imam nouzhda ot ochila.]

I have broken my glasses.
Аз си счупих очилата.
[Az si schoupih ochilata.]
Очилата ми се счупиха.
[Ochilata mi se schoupiha.]

Can you repair them, please?
Можете ли да ги оправите, моля?
[Mozhete li da gi opravite, molya?]

eye	**око** [oko]
eyesight	**зрение** [zrenie]
optical	**зрителен** [zritelen]
	оптически [opticheski]
optician	**оптик** [optik]

PARTS OF THE BODY

ankle	**глезен** [glezen]
arm	**ръка** [ruka]
back	**гръб** [grub]
beard	**мустаци** [moustatsi]
	брада [brada]
blood	**кръв** [kruv]
body	**тяло** [tyalo]
bone	**кост** [kost]
breast	**гръд** [grud]
	гърда [gurda]
chest	**гръден кош** [gruden kosh]
	гърди [gurdi]
chin	**брада** [brada]
ear	**ухо** [ouho]
elbow	**лакът** [lakut]
face	**лице** [litse]
finger	**пръст** [prust]
hair	**коса** [kosa]
hand	**ръка** [ruka]
head	**глава** [glava]
heart	**сърце** [surtse]
kidney	**бъбрек** [bubrek]
knee	**коляно** [kolyano]
leg	**крак** [krak]
lip	**устна** [oustna]
liver	**черен дроб** [cheren drob]
lung	**бял дроб** [byal drob]
mouth	**уста** [ousta]
neck	**шия** [shiya]
nose	**нос** [nos]

shoulder	**рамо** [ramo]
stomach	**стомах** [stomah]
throat	**гърло** [gurlo]
thumb	**палец** [palets]
toe	**пръст на крак** [prust na krak]
tongue	**език** [ezik]
vein	**вена** [vena]
wrist	**китка** [kitka]

WEATHER

What's the weather like today?
Какво е времето днес?
[Kakvo e vremeto dnes?]

It's sunny/cloudy.
Слънчево/облачно е.
[Slunchevo/oblachno e.]

It's warm/cool/cold.
Топло/хладно/студено е.
[Toplo/hladno/stoudeno e.]

It's foggy.
Мъгливо е. [Muglivo e.]

It's raining.
Вали. [Vali.]

It's snowing.
Вали сняг. [Vali snyag.]

Where does the wind come from?
От къде духа вятърът?
[Ot kude douha vyatarut?]

From the north/east/south/west.
От север/изток/юг/запад.
[Ot sever/iztok/yug/zapad.]

What's the temperature?
Каква е температурата?
[Kakva e temperatourata?]

How many degrees is it?
Колко градуса е?
[Kolko gradousa e?]

cloud	**облак** [oblak]
cloudy	**облачно** [oblachno]
cloudy weather	**облачно време** [oblachno vreme]
thunderbolt	**светкавица** [svetkavitsa]
thunderstorm	**буря** [bourya]
weather	**време** [vreme]
fine weather	**хубаво време** [houbavo vreme]
wind	**вятър** [vyatur]

TIME

What time is it?
Колко е часът? [Kolko e chasut?]

At 9 a.m.
В 9. (девет) ч. (часа) сутринта.
[V 9. (devet) ch. (chasa) sutrinta.]

At 8 p.m.
В 8. (осем) ч. (часа) вечерта.
[V 8. (osum) ch. (chasa) vecherta.]
В 20. (двадесет) ч. (часа).
[V 20.(dvadeset) ch. (chasa).]

Around 8 p.m.
Около 20. (двадесет) ч. (часа).
[Okolo 20. (dvadeset) ch. (chasa).]

half	**половин** [polovin]
half an hour	**половин час** [polovin chas]
half past two	**два и половина** [dva i polovina]
hour	**час** [chas]
minute	**минута** [minouta]
quarter	**четвърт** [chetvurt]
quarter of an hour	**четвърт час** [chetvurt chas]

a.m.	**преди обед** [predi obed]
p.m.	**след обед** [sled obed]

It is a quarter to six.
Шест без четвърт е.
[Shest bez chetvurt e.]

It is a quarter past five.
Пет и петнайсет е.
[Pet i petnayset e.]

It is 7:30 p.m.

7 ч. и 30 м. (седем часа и трийсет минути) вечерта е.
[7 ch. i 30 m. (sedem chasa i triyset minouti) vecherta e.]

7 (седем) и половина вечерта.
[7 (sedem) i polovina vecherta.]

19 ч. и 30 м. (деветнайсет часа и трийсет минути).
[19 ch. i 30 m. (devetnayset chasa i triy-set minouti).]

It is early. **Рано е.** [Pano e.]
It is late. **Късно е.** [Kusno e.]

in the morning **сутрин** [soutrin]
in the afternoon **следобед** [sledobed]
in the evening **вечер** [vecher]
at midnight **в полунощ** [v polounosht]

day **ден** [den]
day before yesterday **завчера** [zavchera]
last night **снощи** [snoshti]

today	**днес** [dnes] **днеска** [dneska]
tomorrow	**утре** [outre]
yesterday	**вчера** [vhcera]
four days before	**преди четири дена** [predi chetiri dena]
three days before	**преди три дена** [predi tri dena]
two weeks ago	**преди две седмици** [predi dve sedmitsi]
this week	**тази седмица** [tazi sedmitsa]
last week	**миналата седмица** [minalata sedmitsa]
next week	**следващата седмица** [sledvashtata sedmitsa]
this month	**този месец** [tozi mesets]
last month	**миналият месец** [minaliyat mesets]
next month	**следващият месец** [sledvashtiyat mesets]
this year	**тази година** [tazi godina]
last year	**миналата година** [minalata godina]
next year	**следващата година** [sledvashtata godina]

What day is it today?
Какъв ден е днес?
[Kakuv den e dnes?]

Today is Friday.
Днес е петък. [Dnes e petuk.]

What day will it be tomorrow?
Какъв ден ще е утре?
[Kakuv den shte e outré?]

this morning **тази сутрин** [tazi sutrin]
now **сега** [sega]
at the moment **в момента** [v momenta]

tonight **тази вечер** [tazi vecher]
night **нощ** [nosht]

week **седмица** [sedmitsa]
month **месец** [mesets]
year **година** [godina]

spring **пролет** [prolet]
summer **лято** [lyato]
autumn /fall **есен** [esen]
winter **зима** [zima]

Days of the week

Monday **понеделник** [ponedelnik]
Tuesday **вторник** [vtornik]
Wednesday **сряда** [sryada]
Thursday **четвъртък** [chetvurtuk]
Friday **петък** [petuk]
Saturday **събота** [subota]
Sunday **неделя** [nedelya]

… on Monday
… **в понеделник** [v ponedelnik]

Months of the year

January	**януари** [yanouari]
February	**февруари** [fevruari]
March	**март** [mart]
April	**април** [april]
May	**май** [may]
June	**юни** [yuni]
July	**юли** [yuli]
August	**август** [avgoust]
September	**септември** [septemvri]
October	**октомври** [oktomvri]
November	**ноември** [noemvri]
December	**декември** [dekemvri]

Holidays

Christmas	**Коледа** [Koleda]
Easter	**Великден** [Velikden]
New Year's	**Нова Година** [Nova Godina]

COLORS

black	**черен** [cheren]
blue	**син** [sin]
brown	**кафяв** [kafyav]
green	**зелен** [zelen]
orange	**оранжев** [oranzhev]
purple	**пурпурен** [pourpouren]
red	**червен** [cheren]
violet	**лилав** [lilav]
white	**бял** [byal]
yellow	**жълт** [zhult]

NUMBERS

Cardinal Numbers

one	**един** [edin]
	една[edna]
	едно [edno]
two	**две** [dve]
	два [dva]
three	**три** [tri]
four	**четири** [chetiri]
five	**пет** [pet]
six	**шест** [shest]
seven	**седем** [sedem]
eight	**осем** [osem]
nine	**девет** [devet]
ten	**десет** [deset]
eleven	**единайсет** [edinayset]
twelve	**дванайсет** [dvanayset]
thirteen	**тринайсет** [trinayset]
fourteen	**четиринайсет** [chetirinayset]
fifteen	**петнайсет** [petnayset]
sixteen	**шестнайсет** [shesnayset]
seventeen	**седемнайсет** [sedemnayset]
eighteen	**осемнайсет** [osemnayset]
nineteen	**деветнайсет** [devetnayset]
twenty	**двайсет** [dvayset]
twenty-one	**двайсет и едно** [dvayset i edno]
thirty	**трийсет** [triyset]

forty	**четирийсет** [chetiriyset]
fifty	**петдесет** [petdeset]
sixty	**шейсет** [sheyset]
seventy	**седемдесет** [sedemdeset]
eighty	**осемдесет** [osemdeset]
ninety	**деветдесет** [devedeset]
one hundred	**сто** [sto]
two hundred	**двеста** [dvesta]
three hundred	**триста** [trista]
four hundred	**четиристотин** [chetiristotin]
five hundred	**петстотин** [petstotin]
one thousand	**хиляда** [hilyada]
two thousand	**две хиляди** [dve hilyadi]

Ordinal Numbers

first	**първи** [purvi]
second	**втори** [vtori]
third	**трети** [treti]
fourth	**четвърти** [chetvurti]
fifth	**пети** [peti]
sixth	**шести** [shesti]
seventh	**седми** [sedmi]
eighth	**осми** [osmi]
ninth	**девети** [deveti]
tenth	**десети** [deseti]

MEASUREMENT & CONVERSION

centimeter	**сантиметър** [santimetur]
cm	**см**
gram	**грам** [gram]
g	**г**
kilo	**кило** [kilo]
k	**к**
kilogram	**килограм** [kilogram]
kg	**кг**
kilometer	**километър** [kilometur]
km	**км**
liter	**литър** [litur]
l	**л**
meter	**метър** [metur]
m	**м**
millimeter	**милиметър** [milimetur]
mm	**мм**

Length

1 inch = 2.54 cm	1 cm = 0.39 inches
1 foot = 0.305 m	1 m = 3.28 feet
1 yard = 0.91 m	1 m = 1.09 yards
1 mile = 1.61 km	1 km = 0.62 miles = 5/8 miles

Weight

1 oz = 28.35 g	100 g = 3.5 ounces
1 lb = 0.45 kg	1 kg = 2.2 pounds

Volume

1 U.S. pint = 0.47 liter
1 liter = 2.13 U.S. pints

1 U.S. gallon = 3.79 liter
1 liter = 0.26 U.S. gallons

Temperature

Centigrade/Celsius (**C**)
Fahrenheit (**F**)

C = (F – 32) x 5/9
F = (C x 9/5) + 32

C	**F**
-18	0
-12	10
-7	20
-1	30
4.4	40
10	50
15	60
21	70
26	80
31	90
37	100

www.ingramcontent.com/pod-product-compliance
Lightning Source LLC
Jackson TN
JSHW011356130125
77033JS00023B/706

* 9 7 8 0 7 8 1 8 1 1 3 4 7 *